Routledge Revivals

The Heart of Japan

This collection of commentaries and reflections on Japanese culture, first published in 1904, was written shortly after the return of two English aristocrats from five years spent immersed in the 'Land of the Rising Sun'. Their intention through these anecdotes – some humorous and charming, others tragic and thought-provoking – was to offer glimpses into the "real inner spirit of the native life," and to provide insights into the remarkable idiosyncrasies of Japanese society during a period of unprecedented change.

Touching on such diverse topics as sport, religion, music, censorship, drama and bathing, *The Heart of Japan* will be of particular interest to students of Japanese, as well as to those intrigued by cultural difference and exchange.

The Heart of Japan
Glimpses of Life and Nature Far From the Travellers' Track in the Land of the Rising Sun

Clarence Ludlow Brownell

First published in 1904
by Methuen & Co.

This edition first published in 2014 by Routledge
2 Park Square, Milton Park, Abingdon, Oxon, OX14 4RN
and by Routledge
711 Third Avenue, New York, NY 10017

Routledge is an imprint of the Taylor & Francis Group, an informa business

© 1904 Clarence Ludlow Brownell

All rights reserved. No part of this book may be reprinted or reproduced or utilised in any form or by any electronic, mechanical, or other means, now known or hereafter invented, including photocopying and recording, or in any information storage or retrieval system, without permission in writing from the publishers.

Publisher's Note
The publisher has gone to great lengths to ensure the quality of this reprint but points out that some imperfections in the original copies may be apparent.

Disclaimer
The publisher has made every effort to trace copyright holders and welcomes correspondence from those they have been unable to contact.

ISBN 13: 978-0-415-74134-7 (hbk)
ISBN 13: 978-1-315-81484-1 (ebk)
ISBN 13: 978-0-415-74223-8 (pbk)

THE FAMOUS DRAGON FOUNTAIN

THE HEART OF JAPAN

GLIMPSES OF LIFE AND NATURE
FAR FROM THE TRAVELLERS' TRACK
IN THE LAND OF THE RISING SUN

BY

CLARENCE LUDLOW BROWNELL

WITH TWENTY-FOUR ILLUSTRATIONS

THIRD EDITION

METHUEN & CO.
36 ESSEX STREET W.C.
LONDON
1904

TO
CURTIS BROWN

INTRODUCTORY NOTE

WE lived so far from the travellers' track in Japan,—often where no foreigner had been before,—and had seen and heard so much of what seemed to us humorous, tragic, quaint, or thought-worthy, that we dared to believe sometimes that we were getting glimpses of the real inner spirit of the native life — a spirit far different from that of the tourist-worn borders of this ancient and fascinating Land of the Rising Sun.

Whether or not we are flattering ourselves unduly, the five years that one of us spent in the interior of Japan, sometimes teaching English in the Government schools, sometimes idling, always living as the natives live, were crowded with joyous entertainment

In striving to reproduce some faint tint of this charm, it seemed wisest to present each episode or impression separately—here a personal experience, there a story heard in some peasant's hut or among the temples, or from some old warrior of the feudal days, and again a ventured comment, picturing different phases of the life of Japan, one after another, as on a screen—seemingly detached, perhaps, yet knit together by the underlying desire to present the native point of view.

    JAPAN SOCIETY,
       20 HANOVER SQUARE,
          LONDON, W.

CONTENTS

CHAP.		PAGE
I.	KONO HITO AND THE PRAYER PUMP	1
II.	O TOYO SAN	12
III.	OUR LANDLORD	18
IV.	THE HONOURABLE BATH	28
V.	THE AUGUST DEPARTURE	35
VI.	THE GUEST WHO COULD NOT GO	41
VII.	THE OBEDIENT BED	46
VIII.	ONE WHO WON	56
IX.	THINKING IN JAPANESE	61
X.	BO CHAN	71
XI.	O JO SAMA	83
XII.	HAPPY NEW YEAR	97
XIII.	"CHITS" AND PERDITION	104
XIV.	THE CENSOR AND THE CRAFTY EDITOR	110
XV.	BOBBY	120
XVI.	PLAYHOUSES, PLAYERS, AND PLAYS	124
XVII.	"MUSIC"	134
XVIII.	BLOSSOMS ALWAYS IN BLOOM	139
XIX.	SIGNS OF THE TIMES	145
XX.	BOWS AND BALLOTS	154
XXI.	THE FLOWERS OF TOKIO	158
XXII.	IN THE KINDERGARTEN DAYS	163
XXIII.	IN TRADE	176

CONTENTS

CHAP.		PAGE
XXIV.	DIVING BELLES	187
XXV.	AMONGST THE GODS	194
XXVI.	ON THE EARTHQUAKE PLAN	206
XXVII.	MISSIONARIES AND MISSIONARIES	215
XXVIII.	GILDED WITH OLD GOLD	229
XXIX.	AND SO HE BECAME A SAINT	233
XXX.	KADE AND THE REPEATERS	242
XXXI.	KADE WOULD ADVENTURE	246
XXXII.	WHAT HAPPENED TO ALLEN	249
XXXIII.	THE SPORTSMAN IN JAPAN	260
XXXIV.	THE FATHER OF THE VILLAGE	270
XXXV.	THE THEFT OF THE GOLDEN SCALE	277
XXXVI.	THE KANJI	285
XXXVII.	THE REVERENCE OF KATO	292

LIST OF ILLUSTRATIONS

THE FAMOUS DRAGON FOUNTAIN	*Frontispiece*	
O TOYO SAN'S HOME	*To face page*	12
NICHIYOBI WAS OUR HOME DAY	,,	41
THE GARDENS OF THE OLD TEMPLE	,,	44
THE OBEDIENT BED	,,	50
JAPANESE NURSES CARRY BABIES ON THEIR BACKS	,,	76
THE GAME OF "KITSUNE" FOX	,,	80
"KITSUNE KEN"	,,	82
JAPANESE GIRLS AT HOME	,,	94
A SAMURAI WITH PRISONER	,,	120
GAKUNIN	,,	134
IN JAPAN EVERYONE IS ALWAYS ENTERTAINING SOMEONE	,,	140
A GEISHA	,,	144
SIGNS OF THE TIMES (*A*)	,,	148
SIGNS OF THE TIMES (*B*)	,,	152
TOKIO	,,	160
GOKU TEMPLE	,,	194
THE TERA OR BUDDHIST TEMPLE	,,	196
THE GATEWAY OF THE MIYA, SHINTO TEMPLE	,,	198
AMIDA, THE BUDDHA	,,	202
THE EFFECTS OF AN EARTHQUAKE	,,	212
FIGHTING PRIESTS	,,	227
HERE HIDEYOSHI, THE TAIKO, DRANK HIS TEA	,,	231
NIGHT-FISHING IN JAPAN	,,	268

THE HEART OF JAPAN

CHAPTER I

KONO HITO AND THE PRAYER PUMP

GARDNER and I met Kono Hito the first time we went up the west coast. He was the thriftiest man in Japan. Even taken together we were not his equal. He lived near a temple less than one hundred "ri"[1] from Kanazawa. If he had been farther from the temple he would have been just as close, but he might not have discovered the fact to the world, nor have wasted away on account of his unlovely trait.

Kono Hito was a farmer. Like most native farmers, he raised rice. To do so he had to have water, and plenty of it, enough to cover thousands of "tsubo," as the Japanese say. (A "tsubo" is the size of two mats, or thirty-six square feet.) He owned some fifty fields, lying side by side. They were small and fenceless; only low ridges of earth marked the boundaries of the fields, and these ridges, when the rice had grown, were lost to view. At the time of

[1] 1 ri = about 2½ miles.

planting they would be mushy, but at harvest time they would become dry and hard, so that a man could walk along them easily if he had occasion.

Kono's way of cultivating them was to throw seed rice—that is rice kernels in the shell—over the surface of his ponds, where it sprouted, and wove into a tangled mat of deep, rich green. When the rice blades were six inches long, and had well-formed roots, he would disentangle them, and, gathering them in clusters, would plant them in the mud at two-foot intervals, along rows two feet apart and parallel. This made the rows regular, like the lines of a checker board, with a bunch of rice wherever two lines crossed. The board itself was all water at first, and had to remain water until nearly time for harvest, for Kono Hito grew swamp rice only. He said there was no money in upland rice. It was too hard, and would not sell for the cost of growing it.

A drought, therefore, was about as bad a thing as could happen to Kono Hito. He must have water or go to the money lenders, and once he went to them there would be no end of going until they had possession of his rice-fields. Kono Hito knew the fate of borrowers full well, and to save himself from such calamity he built dams above his fields to make reservoirs, he dug ditches from one field to the other, and he observed the Buddhist fast days. In spite of all this, however, his crops turned yellow earlier than those of his neighbour Sono Hito, the rice grower on the opposite side of the road—a highway that passed between their paddy-fields and led to the temple and beyond.

KONO HITO AND THE PRAYER PUMP

"Komaru domo!" said Kono Hito as he came along this road in his jin-riki-sha one day. "Do shimasho ka?" ("What shall we do?"). But though he spoke to himself of trouble, and asked himself how to avoid it, he did not talk out loud. He sought to succeed by keeping more fast days, working harder in his fields, building tiny shrines, like dolls' houses, at his reservoirs, and bringing the household economy down to such a fine point that Okusama, his wife, dared not lose so much as a grain of rice in a month. But with all his prayers and his skimping, he had not water enough. His fields were brown when Sono Hito's were still green. "Hontoni komaru!" Trouble indeed!

Sono Hito, the meanwhile, was not worrying. He was a patriarch in the "Home of Happy Husbandmen," and never had bad years, even though he kept few fasts and was not more than half careful of his reservoirs.

A lot of folk worked for him, however, and without knowing it, though they were glad in their unconscious service. They were good Buddhists of the Hongwanji sect, passing daily to the grand old temple overlooking the sea. They offered alms to Amida, the Buddha, and ere they offered they washed themselves, as good folk do before they worship. Sono Hito, of course, knew this, for he went himself to the temple sometimes and took the preliminary bath just as the others did. It was while he was taking one of these baths that the idea which resulted in Kono Hito's "komaru" had occurred to Sono San. This is the idea.

Sono's rice-fields reached quite up to the temple grove. He would build a shrine in honour of the temple's god a little this side of the gate of the temple, and near the road. He would sink a well there. It would needs be a deep well, it is true, but Sono's crops had been good and he would not begrudge the cost. Having dug the well he would place a tablet before the shrine, bearing a declaration of the dedication of his offering to the temple's god on behalf of those who worshipped there. He would give each worshipper all the pure water he might desire for a bath, and would not charge him for it. All the worshipper need do would be to pump and help himself! It was a grand scheme, such as only a man who had seen the world could have evolved. Sono had been a traveller.

He knew "Yokohama, Nagasaki, Hakodate, hai," personally, for he had been there. He had seen missionaries in Tokio and merchants in the treaty ports. To one of the missionaries he owed his inspiration. The reverend gentleman had shown him a praying water-wheel from India. It was part of a collection the learned preacher had gathered at various stations he had occupied in the Far East. Sono San delighted in the collection, but the praying-wheel pleased him most. If he had had a place on his west coast rice-fields to set one up he would have begged the missionary to get him one from the ancient home of Buddhism.

Some days after he had seen this supplication-made-simple apparatus, so much simpler than the man-power prayer-wheels of the Tokio temples,

KONO HITO AND THE PRAYER PUMP 5

Sono received an invitation from one of the missionary's friends, a silk merchant in Yokohama. This man wished to make acquaintances on the west coast, especially in Fukui and Kanagawa Kens, where the silkworms spin well. Sono, always ready "to see the new thing," to learn something and to have a good time, took the train at Shimbashi station that afternoon, and within an hour was at "Yama Namban," as the jin-riki-sha coolies called the merchant's house.

Sono Hito had a wonderful time at this foreigner's home. The yoshoku, the setsu-in, the nedai, and the danru, with its kemuridashi, were marvellous to him, but the thing that tickled him especially was what he called the "midzu-age kikai," or water-raising machine, not far from the kitchen door. He played with this a half-hour steadily, until he was all of a sweat and had flooded his host's back yard and turned the tennis-court into a soppy marsh.

Nothing would do but he must have one to operate at his home over on the west coast, and as the kikai was not in stock at any of the Yokohama agencies, Sono Hito's host promised to get one for him from San Francisco.

"I'll send it over to you as soon as it arrives," said Mo-Hitotsu-Smith San. (M. H. S. S. was the second Smith to come to Yokohama after Perry's departure. The first Smith was merely "Smith San," but the second was Mo-Hitotsu-Smith San, *i.e.* more-one-Smith Mr.) He did better than that, however, he took the apparatus over himself three months later, and showed his Japanese friend how to set it up and how he could use it to fill a storage tank so as to have water for emergencies.

So Sono Hito had men dig the well wide and deep. There was not such another well in that part of the country. Kono Hito, across the road, had nothing in the least comparable. He would not have spent so much money on a well had he been never so rich, and in these days he thought himself a very poor man indeed. It grieved him to think that anything that cost money should be necessary in his household. The sight of his people eating made him ill, and the prosperity across the road was like fire against his face. He could not endure to look at it. But as Kono Hito suffered, Sono Hito worked at his well shrine. The building was beautiful in design as anything pertaining to Hongwanji would be. Inside, over at one end, was a broad, shallow, wooden tank for the bather to sit in, and, before the tank, ample floor space, where the worshipper would have room to use his tenugui or scrubbing towel, such as all Japanese carry with them. At the end opposite the tank was the shrine, and beside the tank was a device strange to the natives of the west coast. Sono called it a prayer-machine. Over it was a gaku bearing the Chinese inscription, "Bonno kuno" ("All lust is grief").

An Englishman would not have thought of prayer in connection with this device. He would doubt if the Japanese used water prayer-wheels, and would have said simply "chain-pump." But one may assert with considerable confidence that Englishman or other foreigner never before had seen a chain-pump boxed in an image of Buddha, with a third arm, in the shape of a crank, reaching out from one side and projecting over a bath-tub.

Sono Hito, however, knew all about the apparatus, both from the Yankee and the west coast view-point. He was the only person who did; but, like Brer Rabbit, "he wasn't saying nuffin."

In fact, the two foreigners who did see this device guessed right the very first time, like the young man in the song, but they kept their thoughts to themselves. Sono Hito might call it a prayer-machine, and each bather as he sat in the tub might turn Buddha's third arm with vigour and pray fervently, chanting his petitions in unison with the rat-tat-rat-tat-tattle in Buddha's stomach; to the Yankee's mind the thing would be a chain-pump still.

It was soon after this visit of Mo-Hitotsu-Smith San that the patriarch of the Home of Happy Husbandmen had conceived his scheme of joining piety and prosperity in happy combination by giving faithful Buddhists a cataract bath free and a chance at the prayer-machine thrown in. He had to explain his device, of course, for it was such a noticeable innovation, so he told the village folk that the ancient peoples of China and India had used these machines with august results. He even threw off his kimono, sat himself in the tub and showed them how, after pious revolutions, the Divine Pleasure would give them water from above.

The idea pleased everyone unless it were Kono Hito, for Buddhists are partial to cataract baths. They take them the year round, even in winter, though possibly they do not enjoy them then, at least not with obvious hilarity. In Tokio, the capital, in spite of its modernisation, the traveller sees native men and women standing naked under a fall of water in some of the temple parks. In December and January this water is well down to freezing point. The Japanese do this because they know there is virtue in a cataract. Wherever one is, that place is sacred. If there is none they often take great pains to make artificial falls, especially in the neighbourhood of temples.

They are purifiers beyond all else, these "from-heaven-descending" streams. Therefore, when Sono San made his offer of a free bath—a cataract bath! something the region about the beloved temple had not known since the " O jishin " (the great earthquake), which, hundreds of years before, had broken up the country, letting out the upper waters and ruining their plans of holy ablution—he became the most popular man in the ken.

Sono Hito was deeply grateful to his foreign friend, who had showed him how to rig the pump so as to deliver the water into a tank in the roof of the shrine. This tank was a distributing reservoir. Part of the water that the worshippers pumped into it poured down in a stream on to the head of whoever might be working at the crank, as he or she sat in the tub. The greater part, however, flowed away into channels through the rice-fields. As the

KONO HITO AND THE PRAYER PUMP

pious came, therefore, and worked the prayer-machine, they accomplished three things at once which, in the order of Sono San's idea of their importance, would read—pumping, irrigation, and purification. This explains how Sono Hito kept things green, and why Kono Hito said "Komaru."

Poor Kono Hito worried greatly over the early yellowishness of his fields. He did not understand how Sono Hito managed. He never had been to Yokohama, and he knew nothing of chain-pumps. He believed that Sono Hito's piety had won favour in Buddha's eyes, and that the gods had blessed the fields as a mark of divine pleasure. If he could have a bath shrine he might win favour too, but that would cost money; and then to give the baths free, not to charge even a one-rin[1] piece for them—the thought was too painful.

Still, if Buddha would smile on him, it might pay, thought Kono. It would pay—but to spend the money. "Domo! Komaru ne!" So he devised how he might be pious cheaply.

"Namm Omahen de gisu," said the wife in the dialect of her district when a man called one morning to see Kono Hito. She meant he was not at home (in Tokio she might have said: "Tadaima rusu de gozaimasu." That would have conveyed a similar idea). So the man went away.

Down the road he heard a voice calling "Korario," which to those who live in that region means, "Come here." The man went in the direction of the call, and found Kono Hito busy with a carpenter and

---
[1] One rin equals one-tenth of a farthing.

well-digger, discussing plans for an opposition bath shrine. Kono Hito was in agony over the cost, but the workmen had reached their lowest limit, and, with many bows, were protesting that if they cut their price down even a "mo" further they would not have enough left to pay for the air they breathed while digging. So Kono had to give in.

Within a week the plans had materialised. There was a well with a pair of buckets, a tub, and a shrine dedicated to the use of worshippers. It was not a cataract bath, nor was the well deep, but Kono Hito hoped Buddha would take his poverty into account and smile as sweetly as though the water fell direct from a spring on the mountain side.

But Buddha did not smile. No one went to Kono Hito's shrine bath unless too many had gathered at the place across the way. "Without worshippers Buddha will not smile," said the unhappy husband-man. "Komaru ne!" And later he said to himself, "Do shimasho ka." This brought him inspiration.

He took a station at a point that commanded a view of the road, and whenever he saw those coming who might be worshippers he went into Sono Hito's shrine, sat himself in the tank, turned the crank, and prayed vigorously.

This was a cunning scheme, for the pilgrims, after waiting long for Kono to finish, would decide that such fervent piety should not be disturbed, and, leaving the zealot in Sono Hito's tub, they would cross over to do as best they might with the two buckets. When they had mundificated they emptied these buckets on the roadside. But still Buddha did not smile on the fields of Kono San.

Kono San, however, as he ground and ground away, taking twenty or thirty baths a day, chilling himself in the cataract, and pumping three times as much water over Sono Hito's fields as he brought down on to his aching poll, had much tenacity, and a belief that if he could keep the pious to his side of the road long enough he would receive the blessings his soul yearned for.

He pumped and prayed heroically, resting little and eating less, while Sono Hito took a peep at him occasionally, and showed not the least vexation.

Kono San wondered at this, for he had been rather fearful of discovery, and when he learned that the man he was so jealous of had seen him and had said nothing, he did not understand; nor could he understand why Buddha did not show some sign of favour. As he pumped, he puzzled upon these things, and grew more and more attenuated. Overbathing, even with prayers, is not good.

When Junsa, the policeman, called Isha, the physician, to Sono Hito's shrine one evening, and let his lantern light fall on Kono Hito's face, the man of medicine said, "Water on the brain." Two days later they buried him, and Sono Hito gave money for a stone column to mark the resting-place of the dead man's ashes. Why not? Kono Hito really had helped Sono Hito a good deal.

CHAPTER II

O TOYO SAN

SONO HITO took us over one day to visit his friends at Tatsumi, an interesting old place, where we had a practical demonstration of the irresistibility of Japanese hospitality. We had intended to spend only an afternoon, but our intentions might as well have been non-existent for all that they availed. A wooden image would have succumbed, and neither of us was an image, though, in the light of the native graciousness, we appeared to ourselves wooden enough. So it was that that afternoon visit, under Tatsumi manipulation, expanded into days, and the days into weeks.

We were the only foreigners the villagers had ever seen, and though it was in the days of passports, the police did not ask us to produce our papers. They had never had occasion to look up the law about "barbarians." Tatsumi had given us a chance indeed to see Japan at home. There we were near enough to native life to hear the heart beat. We did not see much of the owner, Hikusaburo, as he was away much, but his father and his mother we came to know well, and also his children,

O TOYO SAN'S HOME.

his doll wife, and last, but far from least, the sweet lady who had preceded her. O Toyo was her name. Once, in Hikusaburo's absence, we paid a three days' visit to her home, a charming place, and again we saw her close to Tatsumi—but not inside.

I recall her now, as she sat tapping the ashes from her silver pipe in one of the small thatched houses that stand just outside the blackened walls of that old homestead. She was waiting for her kurumaya, who had dropped the shafts of his jinriki-sha and was taking a bowl of rice with some old friends at the gate where he had served for so many years. O Toyo San was on her way to Biwa, and farther south, and had stopped at the cottage that she might see her children.

There was a longing in her eyes as she sat half kneeling on the little square mat by the brazier, now arranging the bits of charcoal with her tongs, and now taking a bit of tobacco from the pouch beside her on the matting. Her face was gentle and sweet to look upon. When she smiled her eyes sparkled, and her parting lips discovered pearly teeth that had never needed a dentist's care. But her smile was hardly more than courtesy, despite its gentle look, for there was a yearning in her heart that a woman of another race would hardly have concealed.

She is a mother, but her children are growing up almost as strangers to her. It is not her fault at all. Her parents had arranged her marriage when she was hardly in her teens, without asking her whether she would or not. Obedience was the only law she knew, and with filial piety (why is there not a good Old English equivalent for this term?) she had done her parents' bidding, not questioning their choice. Her lot had been that of many another native woman.

O Toyo San must wait outside to see the children born to her in Tatsumi, a girl and a boy. The boy, O Bo Chan, as the house-folk call him, is heir to the ancient manor. The master of Tatsumi is lord of all the region round. He has owned Hombo, the village extending northward, ever since men first abode there, and the checker-board of rice-fields reaching far out towards the boundaries of Niu Gun, one of the richest counties in the famous province of Echizen.

Those, however, who have long known Tatsumi and the lord thereof doubt if much but the name of these great possessions will be left by the time O Bo Chan has come to man's estate. Bo's grandfather has been "inkiyo" many years. Before he retired from active life to devote himself to study and meditation he had lived like a prince, but well within his income. When he handed over his estates to his son, Hikusaburo, he had accompanied the transfer with much good advice, which the heir had acknowledged dutifully, saying, "Kashikomarimashita" ("I listen with respectful assent"), and "Sayo de gozaimasu" ("Honourably so augustly is") frequently.

But Tatsumi's friends said "Neko ni koban" ("Gold coins to a cat") when they spoke among themselves, though in public they held their peace.

Since then their prophecy has been fulfilling rapidly, but the inkiyo has not paid heed. His cares for this life are over, and his days are sweet and peaceful. O Kamisan, his honoured wife, has seen, but she cannot speak. Indeed she is O Kamisan no longer, only Obasan (grandmother). Her son has become the head of the house, and her duty, as a woman's duty ever is in Japan, is to obey, not to criticise. So Hikusaburo has had free way. Never does anyone say no to him.

His father had given to him O Toyo San before he was done with school. She was the daughter of a rich relation, a saké brewer. The marriage, as is usual in Japan, was purely a family agreement, without civil or religious ceremony, and of course both houses were happy over the event.

When the bride arrived at the home of her new parents, dressed in silken robes, and her face painted white as chalk, the place was thronged with guests. Tatsumi had thrown wide its gates, and there was feasting for a week. Oji San had dispensed clam broth and mushrooms lavishly, and there was joy throughout the whole of Echizen.

Later, when a boy was born, the old walls once more overflowed with joyousness. Oji San smiled at his grandchild, and seeing that it was a healthy babe, put his affairs in order and became inkiyo.[1] Hikusaburo aided him in this, for he was eager to take control. He accepted everything with due humility, even to the patriarchal blessing and advice.

[1] Retired from the management of affairs.

Then he began the life he had longed to lead. His home saw little of him, except when he came in with a band of geisha and made merry till the sun rose. Wherever he went the samisen began to twang, and the moon-fiddle, the koto, and the drum, to fill the air with sounds.

One day Hikusaburo, who was now the father of two children, fell in love. He had been in love before often enough for a day or two; but this time the feeling clung to him, and hurt. Of course she was a geisha, for that was the only sort of woman Hikusaburo had paid attention to since he became lord of Tatsumi. He bought her release from the master who had trained her, and took her home, along with a dozen other of her sisters in the art of spending money. He feared lest she might be lonely.

Tatsumi saw wilder times than ever it had known before. Saké was as plentiful as the rain in June. Hombo hardly recognised itself. O Toyo San, Hikusaburo's wife, only was unhappy. To see herself, the mother of two children, supplanted by a doll not yet fourteen years old, was too much even for her self-abnegation. The cheerfulness which the native code commands to woman was not in evidence in her countenance. Hikusaburo spoke harshly, but she would not brighten up. Then he sent her home. She has not been within the walls of Tatsumi since. She would not enter though not even a ghost were about the place.

So it was when last I saw her that she sat outside waiting while the melancholy music of the samisen floated out from the zashiki, where once she was mistress, and where now my lord made merry with his doll.

The kurumaya said that possibly when my lord was drunk she might see her children.

CHAPTER III

OUR LANDLORD

IT was at Tatsumi that we met Okashi Kintaro, who subsequently became our landlord. He was down from the north on a visit to some friends with whom he had served in his fighting days. We saw him several times, and so enjoyed the enthusiasm he displayed at various feastings, to which we had the good luck to receive invitations, that we besought him to let us go along with him a way on his return.

"Too happy," he assured us. Such an honour he would not have dared to hope for. And so with mutual satisfaction we started on the journey up the coast.

He was a triumph as a guide, for he knew all the interesting folk along the route, and presented us to the "choja" or headman, of each village we passed through. Literally we had to eat our way. On the last day, which was the hardest, we had nine banquets. We were in Okashi's native country by this time, and, as we learned later, he had advertised our coming with a showman's zeal. Such schools as were in session closed, and the villagers

OUR LANDLORD

turned out *en masse* to see "the red whiskers" and "the man with green eyes" (all eyes that are not brown are "green" in Japanese, and beards that are not black are "red"). We fancied ourselves Crown Princes on a tour, but the truth was we were only curiosities.

I shall never forget the breakfast of that last day. It was at the house of a well-to-do farmer, Hyakusho Sama, a friend of Okashi's, where we had supped and spent the night. While serving us our host had noticed that we liked a certain walnut sweet particularly, and so the good wife had sat up all the night making more of it for our breakfast. I had never eaten walnut sweet for breakfast before, and I think I never shall again. To be sure, it was only a side dish, but host and hostess urged us so often to eat some of it that we began to believe that it was the only thing on the floor that they wished us to eat. This notion was quite wrong, however, for there was the regular breakfast of custards, salted plums, mushrooms, fish, and rice. These were served in courses on tiny wooden trays of lacquered wood, and in cups and bowls that would have made a collector transgress the tenth commandment.

I should say, too, as I recall the appearance of the floor whereon we sat, that the hostess had brought in a regular dinner complete, after each course of the breakfast, for I counted over ninety dishes in front of Hyakusho, Okashi, Gardner and me, and many bottles besides. The largest dishes held the walnut sweet, more than I should have cared to carry in a handbag, to say nothing of my interior, but Hyakusho's wife was keen, and laid our disinclination to eat these walnut slabs to our modesty. This modesty she endeavoured to overcome, and was so assiduous in her urging that we made great effort to comply. We munched and munched and munched, mechanically and unhappily, until at last our hostess purred—but, oh dear!

Though some years have passed since that morning at Hyakusho Sama's house, the muscles of my jaws ache now whenever I think of the work I did. Our efforts to please the good wife put us in rather bad form for the series of functions Okashi had devised for our progress into his domain. Our faces pained us so we could not even ruminate, nevertheless we had to take part in eight more banquets, each of them much like the first except for the walnut sweet. Had that appeared again that day I should not have written of our journey —there would have been no time. I should have "passed on," and, being in a Buddhist country, should have been duly reincarnated, doubtless as a huge green walnut for little boys to throw things at.

The ninth banquet was at Okashi San's own home. I do not remember anything about it. We were in the capital of Etchiu, on the west coast of Dai Nippon, looking out over the North Sea, as they call it there, toward the frozen Siberian coast. Here Okashi Kintaro had a charming home, however, a dutiful son, and a good thing. We were the good thing. We rather enjoyed being a good thing — that is, we did after we had recovered;

the experience was so interesting. Okashi was a samurai of the old school, brought up under the feudal system. He knew how to fight, of course, as all gentlemen should in those days. If he knew anything else he concealed it during the year we lived with him. I do not count his knowledge of how to make merry — to "paint the town red," so that his evening environment looked as if it had been lacquered with the hues of the setting sun; for such knowledge was not remarkable. Every samurai in Japan could do that, not to mention humble folk. He was quite regardless of expense in this employment, being of gentle birth, and, besides, he had no money. It is true the Government had pensioned him when it abolished the feudal system and "caste," doing away thereby with samurai as a class, but that pension was mortgaged. Okashi Kintaro had spent forty years of it in advance.

At this time, thanks to what was known as "the most favoured nation clause" in Japan's treaty with the chief countries of the world, and to general bungling in the Department of Foreign Relations, outsiders could neither own nor rent property in their own names, except in restricted districts of some half-dozen cities, such as Tokio, Yokohama, Kobe, Osaka, Nagasaki, Niigata, and Hakodate. As we wished to study Japanese life, we did not care to live in any of the foreign concessions, where one never is quite in touch with real Japan. So we had come to the west coast, to a province where no foreigners had lived before; and as we could not be our own landlord, we proceeded to hire one. Okashi San then seemed just the man, and we thought ourselves in great luck to secure him.

So it was that when we asked him to be our landlord, he hailed the idea with delight. He said he liked foreigners, and confided in a friend, as we discovered, that he considered young ones were better than a pension. It is only fair to say that he was brave whenever there was occasion, and exceedingly generous when he had anything to give. Often he put himself to great personal inconvenience to do one a favour.

According to our agreement we hired him to hire us as instructors in a school that offered wonderful facilities for teaching the English language. Okashi rented two beautiful old temples that had flourished in the Shogun's time under his bounty, but now were empty. One was for the school and one for our living-house. He lived with his family in the school, and for the first month his wife cooked for us, and both of them did our marketing. At the end of the month we called for the bills. Okashi San would not hear of it. "Iye, iye!" ("No, no!") he would repeat. "August pardon deign, but the school is a resplendent success, and I and my stupid wife are overwhelmed with honour. It is we who owe you."

This went on for three days, until we began to believe Okashi meant it, so we proceeded to put out money to other uses. When it had thus been put, he appeared before us one warm afternoon with a roll of thin brown paper exactly nineteen feet six inches in length. (We measured it along the edge of the "tatami."[1]) It was a bill. Okashi San made a bow for every foot in the strip, and then began to read it to us. It was an object lesson in Japanese minuteness of detail.

Many of the items were in fractions of a farthing. One for pepper was 0.0153 or, as the Japanese read it, "kosho is sen, go rin, sam mo." Gardner said the sam mo ($\frac{3}{100}$ of a farthing) was unnecessary extravagance, as we could have had quite enough for an even "is sen go rin. Three decimals was deep enough to go into such hot stuff as pepper."

Okashi bowed eight times and said, "Sayo de gozaimasu," which we interpreted gratefully to imply that next month there would be economy in condiments. When the reading was over we learned that the footing of the nineteen feet was four guineas, or a little over fourpence an inch. This was a surprise, for we had expected nothing less than twenty pounds, estimating by the length of time it took to read from the beginning to the end. As we had not four guineas, Gardner wired a friend in Tokio and received six pounds the next morning. We paid Okashi San the four guineas, and he returned in half an hour with a red seal and a stamp at the end of his scroll, showing that the bill had been duly paid. We asked him if he was sure everything had been settled for, as his bringing in a bill after so many protestations had not pleased us, and we wished to clean our slate entirely while we were about it.

[1] The mats on a native floor. They measure 6′ × 3′.

"Indeed that is all," said our landlord. "It is everything, even the rent."

Upon this we devised how we should disburse what was remaining out of the six pounds. We decided to study the famous "No" dancing, the most ancient of all Japanese ceremonies, and our money disappeared pleasantly.

The next day as we sat on the tatami, wondering if we should ever learn what to do with our legs—most inconvenient appendages in rooms that have no chairs—the "karakami"[1] slid apart and Okashi Okusama appeared, bowing multitudinously. She had a roll of thin brown paper in her hand, like the one her husband had brought in, and she pushed it gently towards us as she bowed.

"We squared all that up yesterday," said Gardner.

"Sayo de gozaimasu, O chigai masu de gozaimasu," said Okusama.

"'Honourably different augustly is,' is it?" asked Gardner. "I don't think so. Let's see it." And he unrolled it along the tatami edge.

"By Jove! you've added two feet," he exclaimed. "And where's the stamp and the seal?"

"Shiremasen de gozaimasu" ("Not knowing augustly am"), said Okusama.

After a lengthy discussion we discovered that the twenty-one feet and six inches bill was a separate account, quite distinct from her husband's and as just. Gardner had to wire to Tokio for another six pounds.

We got into such a mess trying to straighten out

---

[1] Sliding doors of paper, which are the partition walls between rooms.

this second account, which persisted in mixing itself up with account number one, that we decided to hire a professional cook and to let him pay cash for everything as we went along. We gave him his money day by day, and so escaped monthly bills. This really lightened the work of our landlord and landlady greatly, but they disapproved the change, nevertheless; it had been such a joy ordering things at the various shops about town.

After this affairs went on smoothly for some time, until one morning Okashi San handed Gardner a slip of paper on which appeared the following items: Raw fish, mushrooms, eggs, saké, Mlle. Cherry Blossom, Peach Bud, Chrysanthemum, Golden Plum, and Thousand Joys—a combination that suggested gaiety. (Not long before the public had voted for Thousand Joys in the newspapers, and had elected her Grand Mistress of the geisha by a large majority.) As our home and the school had been quiet the night before, we did not understand Okashi's slip. He explained, however. Some dear friends were leaving Etchiu for a long journey, and he had been saying "good-bye." As he had no money he brought the bill to us. He had had a jolly time and was sorry we had not been with him; he would have asked us, but his friends, being strangers, might have been unamusing.

Under the circumstances, Gardner had nothing to do but go into his sleeve for the amount of the bill. In the evening when he had recovered somewhat, he made remarks about oriental "cheek."

We had another example of this cheek later, after

we had laid aside our foreign attire in Etchiu, had put on the native Japanese dress, and adopted the native manner of living in everything else as well. A large part of our discarded clothes we gave to Okashi San and to his son Kojiki. They took the suits to the tailor's and had them cut down to fit. Kojiki San took advantage of this opportunity of giving orders, and told Shitateya San, the tailor, to make a neat cutaway coat with a waistcoat to match. We hardly knew him when he presented himself in his new attire and handed us the bill for all the tailoring. He said he would like some new patent leather boots, too, to wear with the suit, but to his sorrow Shitateya San could not make them. We allowed him to wait for the boots.

On another occasion Gardner went to Niigata to see some naval friends, and while he was there I ran out of funds and wired him for twelve pounds. He and a friend each sent six pounds. It so happened I was called over the mountains before the reply came, and was gone three days on business connected with the Government schools. When I returned I heard from afar the wail of a Japanese song. The voice sounded familiar, and on going into the house I found Okashi San on his back in some ashes near an American stove we had set up in one of the schoolrooms. His legs and arms were in the air, and he was singing a Japanese song of Gardner's composition: "Doitashi mashite abunaio isakijitsu go men na sai," etc. Noisy, but altogether meaningless. When he saw me he jumped up and did an old samurai war-dance, explaining the while that the twelve pounds had come all right, and that he had taken my seal and got the money from the telegraph office.

He had not eaten anything, he said, for three days; but saké!—ah! ah! and he showed a snow-white tongue. Then he untwisted his obe[1] and handed me one and sixpence, all that remained of the money Gardner and his friend had wired. He said he had paid many bills and had enjoyed himself, but we never learned exactly where the money went to, though we had suspicions.

When Gardner decided to resign his professorship and to leave Japan, there was sorrow in Etchiu. The great folk of the province visited the house and brought him testimonials and gifts. Together these presents made a beautiful collection. About half an hour before Gardner's jin-riki-sha was to start, Okashi Kintaro came over with a glorious red bowl which he gave with many protestations of undying regard. Then he "borrowed" three pounds.

[1] Girdle.

CHAPTER IV

THE HONOURABLE BATH

GARDNER made a study of baths while he was in Japan. What he did not know about them when he left the country was exactly enough to make him a native bathing-suit. It is odd, too, that he should have taken to the "furo oke" so enthusiastically when one recalls his first experience in a Tokio bath-tub.

This is what he told some globe-trotters at the Yokohama United Club one day. They were asking for points on "doing" Japan.

"I had just run up to Tokio to see a man in the Imperial University," he explained. "He wasn't at home, but a young student who was taking care of his place greeted me most hospitably. He said: 'Oh, you are just from a long voyage and have a letter for the professor. I am a thousand times sorry that he is not at home. He has gone to Nikko for a period of two weeks. But come in, nevertheless. I am a most stupid and contemptible substitute, but I shall do my idiotic best to explain Japan to you.'

"He made a noble beginning, I assure you. The first lesson was chopsticks. He taught me so well

THE HONOURABLE BATH

that I was expert in half an hour. Then he fed me with seaweed and raw fish. I'll tell you about that later. And finally he boiled me. I am perfectly serious—he boiled me. This is how it was.

"The custom here, you know, is to bathe every afternoon. My young friend's bath-tub was out on the lawn. It was the regulation Japanese tub, an oval arrangement about as high as it is long and a foot longer than it is wide. In one end there is a stovepipe running down through the bottom. The top of this pipe is just even with the rim of the tub. At the bottom there is a grate which holds the charcoal fire that heats the water. The idea is to get into the tub when the water is warmed a little and then sit there while the temperature rises gradually. This rising process is most effective.

"The Japanese can stand it until the thermometer shows 125 to 128 degrees. So can I, now, after I've been at it a year, but it's something to be worked up to gradually. The first time you try a Japanese bath, 95 degrees will do much better. I was a little shy at first about going on the lawn, but, as there was no one except the student in sight, I ran out and jumped into the tub. It was fine! the blue sky overhead and the wide, wide world around me. 'This is luxury,' I said, 'I shall apply for naturalisation papers to-morrow and settle down for the rest of my life in Japan. I would not leave this for heaven' (later on I thought of another place). And so I sat there thinking of the things I should do in this perfect land, and of the fun doing them would be.

"But while I was musing the fire burned. I didn't

notice it at first; not until I observed something else. That was that this young student's wife and her maid had come out while I was in my tub and were busy washing rice by the well, not far away. 'That's extraordinary inadvertence,' I said to myself, or words to that effect; 'why didn't that bally rat tell them that I was out here in the tub? I'd like to wring his neck! They'll be gone soon, I hope!' But I was hot. So was the water, and it grew hotter! 'They're not in a hurry with that rice,' I remarked. 'Confound a country where it takes them all day to wash rice!' I'd forgot about its being heaven, you see. Then I said harsh things—inwardly, of course—but it did no good. It didn't cool the water, nor me, a bit.

"The water behaved badly. It didn't warm up gradually to the boiling point, thereby allowing me to simmer into mock missionary broth. It 'het' itself up by jerks. It would simmer gently, then drop about two degrees, just enough to fool me into the idea that the fire was going out, and that I should be comfortable, and then it would buck up six points, and I'd have a touch of Hades.

"And still they washed that rice. If I could have yelled I'd have felt better, but I was afraid. I thought they would turn round and see me. Then I tried to sneak to the house, but just as I'd be half-way out, one of them would look round, or look as if she were going to look round, and down I'd duck. Every time I dropped I felt my hide peel off, just as in the stories they used to tell of fellows being skinned alive in the Western Plains by Injuns.

"All the water was too hot, but at the surface it felt like a red-hot ring bound to my body. I tried to stir it up to equalise the heat, but motion was painful. I felt as if I couldn't move. I hadn't enough resolution. You see, I was nearly done. So I braced my feet against the little partition that serves as a fender to the iron pipe, and tried to endure it. The water grew hotter, and I braced harder, until there was a crack and a splash. The fender gave way, and my foot went plumb against the sizzling pipe.

"It was just then that I forgot all about the clothes that I didn't have on. I also forgot about the rice washers, and that they could see me. I forgot everything, in fact, except that I was boiled almost to death. As I jumped, I slipped backward on the edge of the tub, rolled round on the back of my neck for a second or two, though it seemed like as many hours, got my feet on the ground at last, and then rushed into the house just in time to meet two American missionary ladies, who had called not knowing that the professor was out of town.

"They didn't seem to be shocked. I had sense enough left to notice that. Afterwards I heard that one of them had remarked how red I was. Well, I was embarrassed."

After a boy had seen to certain orders, Gardner continued: "Now, if you fellows want to get at the real Japan—Japan *au naturel*—be sure and take plenty of baths while here. The bath is the best point of view that you can find to study human nature from. Don't listen to what anyone tells you in the treaty ports; not, at least, till you have made a tour of the country and have taken at least one thousand baths. Then let the folk you meet in Kobe, Yokohama, and Nagasaki tell you all they know, and you will understand them.

"Some of the foreign residents can give you many points, but others will supply misinformation. Wait till you've had your baths before you judge. Japan as seen from the bath-tub is the real Japan. If you don't know enough to write a book when you come back it will be because you were struck blind early in the visit. You'll have chances for your camera, too, and you must work at your sketch-book perpetually. Take notes, and come back ripe for fame.

"It is remarkable that no one has yet 'written up' Japan from the bath-tub side. Even Lafcadio Hearn, who is more sympathetic than anyone else, so far, among the men who write about the country, pays small attention to the tub. Basil Hall Chamberlain, however, who is a mine of learning, has something to say on the subject. He tells of the bathers at Kawara-yu, near Ikao, who stay in the tub a month at a time, with stones in their laps to keep their bodies from floating when they are asleep. He says the tub is one of two things the Japanese haven't borrowed from other countries. The other is their poetry. It hardly would be worth your while to go in for the poetry to any extent. It would take you five years to learn to read it, and twice as long to learn to compose it yourself. But with hot baths it is different. You can learn to take them in a few weeks; if you will profit by my experience, do not begin too hard or be too shy. As I said before, your native friends are likely

THE HONOURABLE BATH 33

to be in water at 115 degrees to 120 degrees, that would take the hide right off a beginner. I got so tough after a few months' practice that I could sit still in water at 125 degrees. I couldn't move round, of course, and I had to be very slow getting in and out, but I could stand the heat even on my face.

"If I were you I'd get a student from the university to act as guide. He would be trustworthy, and would be good company too. Don't have anything to do with the professional guides at the treaty ports. They'll take all sorts of advantage of you. When you've found a student that speaks English well—and most of them do, though in an amusingly formal way—start off for the west coast. Travel the unfrequented routes as much as possible, by that I mean routes that foreigners do not take. You can find hundreds of charming places that few foreigners have seen. And in many of these places there are hot springs and mineral baths. You must see some of the more frequented baths, of course, such as Atami, Hakone, Ojigoku, and Kusatsu, even if they are on beaten paths.

"If any of you fellows have rheumatism or gout go to Kusatsu, 4000 feet up and about thirty miles from Ikao. Kusatsu will cure everything but love-sickness. That is the burden of the song the maids who rub your back and take charge of your kimono sing to you while you bathe. Always watch the people about you. You'll see everyone in the neighbourhood every day—villagers and the visitors alike, men and women, young and old, large and small, every morning and evening. All come into the village square, disrobe, and let themselves down gently into the huge tank of running water.

"Then the news of the day and the gossip of the neighbourhood are discussed from every view point. Listen hard, and have your guide mix up in the talk as much as possible. Get him to repeat to you all that he remembers after the bath is over. Don't talk to him in the bath, or the neighbours will crowd round to hear the queer sounds you make. They will stop talking of their own doings, which are what you wish to become familiar with, and will talk about your skin and hair and eyes, how large you are, and all that sort of thing. When you go back to your hotel you can have a lesson in Japanese from your guide, and incidentally teach him a little English, which is what he's really after.

"One reason why these baths are good for studying native life is, that they are the only places where the sexes come together for general conversation. The Government says that the presence of women keeps the men from talking politics too much, and though missionaries say that the custom is shocking, the Government does not interfere. 'We have been bathing this way for two thousand years without scandal, why should we change?' the natives say; 'there is no evil in the custom to those whose minds are free from evil.' So they ignore the pleadings of the 'sky pilots,' and the children of Japan continue bathing in just the sort of suits they wore when they were born."

CHAPTER V

THE AUGUST DEPARTURE

"SPEAKING of feasts and funerals," said Gardner to the men who had listened to his words on "bath," and were sitting with him at One Hundred Steps the following day, "I saw an old man roasting while his family sat round eating and drinking and making merry. It was over on the west coast, where cremation is much in vogue.

"It was a strange sight to me, for I had not been in the country long and did not know anything about the native funeral customs. The old man who was burning had been our neighbour. He was Okashi's father. That is how I happened to be at the funeral.

"He was eighty-eight years old. This is the lucky age in Japan, because of the way the number is written." Then Gardner made marks on the top of his tray with his chopsticks dipped in shoyu—two little dabs pointing up at each other for eight; then, below, a cross for ten; and below this two more little dabs. The column then read eight, ten, eight. "Now if the four dabs were brought close to the cross in the middle, the eighty-eight would change into the character "rice." The dabs representing hulled kernels, and the cross, a bit of the sieve, the symbol for plenty, so the man or woman reaching the age of eighty-eight is held in particular esteem, and my friend's funeral was more elaborate than the usual affair because of his lucky age.

"Crowds came to the house, for everybody that knew anybody knew Takaiyanagi Inkiyo. They came in and bowed before the household shrine, where his name and the age of such good omen were inscribed. As they bowed they pressed their hands together as Christians do in prayer. They reverenced his spirit, and by their obeisance they implied that they held his memory in as high esteem as they had held him when he was a living man. But they did not worship, as some folk would wish to have you believe. Then they laid their offerings on the floor below the little image in its gilded case. Everyone brought something. The well-to-do gave money, others cakes or wine, and others bamboo vases full of flowers. Some of these were red and some were white.

"Meanwhile the good wife of the house was busy in the kitchen preparing food for the guests. In neighbouring kitchens, too, the women helped with this. In my house cooking began early in the morning, and the maids kept at it all day long. When the cooking was over there was more food than ever I saw before: raw fish, sugared fish, cuttle-fish, seaweed soups, and cold boiled rice rolled up in seaweed, with a dab of horse-radish in the centre.

"The feasting lasted till noon next day, when it

THE AUGUST DEPARTURE

was time for the ceremony to begin. Priests came from an Hongwanji temple near at hand, and saw the old man's body put away properly into a jar shaped like a huge flower-pot, with fragrant leaves pressed in round about it. Then they stood the jar over in the corner for the night, and covered it with a white cloth, so that it looked quite like a bit of furniture sewed up for the summer.

"When all was ready for the procession the next day, the mourners put the jar into a white box, and placed the white cloth over it as before (white is the mourning colour in Japan), and some white-robed attendants from the temple carried it off on a stretcher on their shoulders.

"Just ahead of the jar walked a company of singers with bells. They were in white also, in fact we were all in white except Okashi Kintaro. He had on a wonderful dress-suit, made, after the foreign pattern, much too large for him, and lined with pink silk. The trousers, which he had rolled up some eighteen inches on each leg, fitted as though they were on 'hind side first.' His hat was odd, too. It was of the good old stove-pipe design, straight at the sides, with a broad and flat brim. It was fortunate for Okashi that he had ears, or his hat would have dropped down on to his shoulders. Altogether there was a homelessness and lonesomeness in his appearance as he ambled along in this outfit that was as distressing as it was amusing. I had the honour to be in the procession too. I wore a white duck suit, white canvas shoes, and a white helmet, and rode in a jin-riki-sha.

"At the temple the bearers put the jar on an altar, and a dozen priests chanted a service. While the chanting went on, each guest stepped forward in turn, and, after bowing to the priests, knelt before the bier, and salaaming quite to the floor, took a pinch of powdered incense from a bowl and dropped it into a charcoal brazier, in which a tiny fire burned. Then with another prolonged salaam the mourning guest returned to his seat. This was a sort of 'good-bye' to the body and a salutation to the spirit of the ancient gentleman.

"When my turn came I was so awkward as to put my fingers into the brazier, thereby burning them, and then, in confusion, I put too much incense on the fire, which made such a smoke that the priests and I had a coughing fit.

"Afterwards I explained that we always did that way at home. We burned our fingers a little to purify them, and the last man always dumped on all the incense that was left so that the corpse wouldn't think we were ungenerous. Since then I have been regarded in Etchiu as one learned in holy things.

"After this ceremony and the sneezing was over we took the dead man to a crematory, the only kind of building in Etchiu that has a chimney. Fire was already burning under the oven, and the younger priests were setting a banquet more elaborate, if possible, than had been served at the house. At one side stood several tall vases of pure white porcelain full of saké, and, near these, stacks of shallow drinking-cups of red lacquer.

"We seated ourselves on small cushions laid about on the soft matted floor. I sat like the others, kneeling on my heels. Okashi San protested much. 'You are a foreigner,' said he, 'and are doing me such an overwhelming honour by coming here to-day that I cannot reconcile myself to the idea of your placing your august body in a position so uncomfortable. We Japanese are used to it. Augustly condescend to act in accordance with the request which I have had the gross effrontery to make!' I persisted, however, in sitting native fashion, and had cramps in each leg afterwards, much to the amusement of the other guests.

"Just then the priests took the body from the jar, and, having wrapped it carefully in white, they put it on an iron grating and slid it far back into the furnace, though where all could get a good view of it. The flames curled round it fiercely at first and then almost tenderly, as though caressing it. Now and then they would lash furiously and tie themselves in fantastic knots about the limbs, which bent and unbent and quivered as though life were not yet extinct and they could feel the terrible heat.

"So while the venerable departed writhed and roasted in the flames, we banqueted. It was gruesome, I confess, especially when one of the old man's family would go to the oven and turn him over with an iron rod to 'do' him better on the other side, or would straighten him out so that the fire could get at him better. I had always been in favour of cremation, but I'll be hanged if I liked sitting there watching a man kink up and sputter while his relatives turned him as a chef turns things on a grill.

"I had recourse to saké to steady my nerves. Saké is about the strength of sherry, so that if you drink enough of it, especially hot saké, you will produce an effect. I produced one in the crematory. Every time any of the guests offered me a cup, I took it, and poured the contents into me. It is the custom to exchange cups, you know. You rinse your cup in a bowl of water provided for that purpose and offer it to each guest in turn. You must do this once at least to everyone present, and you always receive a cup in return. There were twenty-nine of us at the funeral, and I had two drinks with each of them!

"I told my host that, when my time came, he must see that I was properly cremated. He replied that it would be too great an honour for him. 'You had much better come to cook me,' he said. Finally, we decided that which ever 'augustly departed' first, the other should burn him, and that the town should have saké enough to swim in. We agreed, however, not to die before we were eighty-eight.

"'Just see how beautifully my father burns,' Okashi San said. 'That is because of his lucky age.' 'Wait till you see me sizzle,' I replied, 'you will be amazed. I intend to go off like a keg of powder.'

"Had either of us caught fire that afternoon he would have burned with a blue flame."

NICHIYOBI WAS OUR HOME DAY

CHAPTER VI

THE GUEST WHO COULD NOT GO

JAPANESE callers come early and stay late—particularly if you, the callee, are a foreigner. They like to look at you. They are easy enough to entertain, too, if you do not mind being stared at. But they never go. At least no one but Dara Santaro ever went, and he did so only once. He could not do so again, for he did not come back. This achievement of his (which was partly ours) emphasises the rule. Here is the story.

Dara Santaro was in the habit of calling on us on Nichiyobi regularly. Nichiyobi is the seventh day of the Japanese week, and corresponds to our Sunday, though it has nothing to do with religion. It is rather jollier and happier than other days, that is all. Gardner and I had enjoyed it in peace and restfulness until Dara discovered us.

Nichiyobi was our home day. We were satisfied to be by ourselves. It was always a comfort in anticipation and a delight when it arrived. But Dara changed all that. He was the nephew of our next-door neighbour, a retired naval captain, who, though a cripple, was courteous and kindly in the extreme. Moreover, he spoke a little English, which made him the more agreeable, whereas Dara did not know more than three words.

When Dara made his first call we were still snoozing on our "futon,"[1] and he had bowed twelve times before we had got the kinks out of our necks sufficiently to bow back to him. Japanese pillows are excellent, once one is used to them; but they are hard on the neck the first few years. Usotsuki, a young student who interpreted for us, said Dara was extremely sorry to disturb us. Dara's sorrow was manifested by a smile that divided his countenance into hemispheres. Our own sorrow was as intense, but different.

We told Kintaro to make Dara comfortable and to excuse us for a moment. Then we rolled out of our "nemaki"[2] and into our boiling bath. When we came out we were red, and breakfast was ready. Dara sat with us on his shinbones and heels, with his feet crossed under him, and nearly added another inch to his smile in an effort to eat an olive with his knife. We did not care much for olives for breakfast, but Usotsuki had put them on the table and Dara San seemed to like them.

Generally, too, we discarded knives and forks and ate with hashi like the natives, but this morning we brought out the English implements, thinking they might interest our guest. They did. He ate everything, even butter, which is not usual among the Japanese. Indeed, he speared the balls floating in the bowl of iced water and swallowed them with

[1] Heavy quilts.   [2] Kimono for sleeping.

THE GUEST WHO COULD NOT GO

an indrawn hiss, like the sound of a small skyrocket. He continued to eat until there was nothing left but the utensils and a bottle of tabasco sauce. He wept over that.

When Dara had done complimenting us he smiled and said, " O gotso sama." From Usotsuki's previous explanation, which seemed founded on antithesis, we judged that Dara was once more expressing sorrow. Perhaps he had a stomach-ache. We were not surprised that he should have one. But no, we had misjudged his smile a second time.

"He say very glad too much eatings," Usotsuki explained.

"We did not know he was coming or we might have prepared," Gardner remarked. This seemed to please Dara greatly when it was translated to him, and he said he would come again next Nichiyobi. Gardner told him to come any day he liked, but Dara replied that official duties hindered him except on that one day.

Then he sat and sat, we the meanwhile wondering what to do for him. We showed him all our foreign photographs. These interested him, and he did us the honour to ask for the only pictures of our families that we possessed. He smiled when we said they were altogether too unworthy for us to think of presenting them to an august guest, but he had a puzzled look about the eyes.

Then we showed him some books on Japan, over which he chuckled like an infant. After that we took some snapshots of him. The minute he faced the camera his smile turned to haughtiness, and he looked like a brazen image, which is the proper Japanese pose; but when he saw the negative in our dark room a little later he was tickled. We promised to send him proofs in a few days, and he bowed and smiled, and stayed.

Usotsuki announced tiffin—always an elaborate meal with us on Nichiyobi. Dara San stayed, and was as active as at breakfast. His compliments were loud and long. As we were fond of his uncle we said nothing, but we were eager for "our Sunday." We wanted to lounge and stroll about the gardens of the old temple in which we lived, and over into the older temple which we were using as a school-house. We wanted to chat together of things at home, to finish our letters and be at rest. But there were none of these things for us this day, nor the following Nichiyobi either, for he remembered the promise which we had quite forgotten.

That second day of visitation was not a keen delight. Then came a third and a fourth. What should we do? We could not be rude. Not for a year's rent would we have disturbed that kindly gentleman the captain. We did not wish to flee. We wanted to have our home to ourselves this one day in the week. We must resort to strategy. And, in fact, to use a slang expression, we must put up a job on Dara Santaro. Though outwardly polite and friendly, we had concocted and concealed in our hearts a wicked scheme. It was done in this wise—

As everyone knows, saké is the national drink of Japan. It is a pale sherry-coloured liquor or beer, made of rice. It is joyous and harmless, though

THE GARDENS OF THE OLD TEMPLE

THE GUEST WHO COULD NOT GO 45

exhilarating to the Japanese. Foreign liquors, like foreign tobacco, are too strong for them. Dara knew nothing of this, however.

After tiffin No. 4, we tried some foreign cigarettes on him, which he smoked until he was a little dizzy. "Tabaka yota" (Tobacco drunk) the natives call the sensation. Then we gave him some of our saké highly sweetened. He had a curiosity to taste the foreign product, and, like all Japanese, he liked plenty of sweetness.

We loaded his tumbler with syrups, but also with liquors, and, I fear, nearly three fingers of "fire water," for it was a tall English glass, holding almost a pint. Our glasses held a mixture of the same in colour, but innocent of dynamite.

Our deception was base but successful. Dara smacked his lips and smiled half-way round his head over the first swallow. His face reddened as he continued to imbibe, but he persisted with the courage of a sentenced feudal lord in the days of "hara-kiri." By the time he had drunk all, his head stuck up through the top of his kimono like a poppy and his smile was saggy at the ends.

He articulated, "Taihen uroshi, gochiso sama, gomen na sai, syonara,"[1] and then sailed sweetly, with many curves, out through our garden, his kimono following like a comet's tail, and his geta playing leap-frog and filling the air with their wooden clamour.

Though we have felt guilty ourselves, we have never blamed Dara Santaro that he did not return.

[1] Very good! Great feast, sir!! August pardon deign!!! Good-bye!!!!

CHAPTER VII

THE OBEDIENT BED

GARDNER and I took a vacation of some three weeks, and leaving Okashi and the west coast made a hurried trip to Tokio. When we reached there the city seemed fearfully European—such was the effect of a few months' experiences across the Empire. Tokio was now as strange for its foreign features as it had been formerly for its native characteristics. We were being Japanned.

We ran into some friends who were staying at the Imperial Hotel, and they led Gardner into a discourse on glimpses of native life. He began with the bed, which is the starting-point of Japanese, as well as foreign, life, and the finishing point too.

"In Japan," he said, "you don't go to bed; the bed comes to you. It is much easier that way, and in Japan the easiest way is the only way. That is why the country is so popular with globe-trotters. Nor does it make much difference what part of your house you may be in, or of a friend's house, for that matter, or a tea-house or an hotel; if you are drowsy the bed will come in patty-pat, and will spread out before you at a moment's notice.

"If you are visiting, your host will detect your inclination and beg you to honour his house by taking a nap therein. Clapping his hands, he calls out: 'Futon motte koi' ('Quilts bring!') In a moment his wife is prostrate just outside the room, hearkening to the august command. In two minutes she will be toddling in with a bundle in her arms much larger than herself—a huge, thickly wadded quilt, the 'futon,' which she rolls out over the 'tatami,' the straw mattresses covered with finely woven bamboos that are upon all floors in Japanese rooms (excepting only the 'daidoku,' or kitchen). That is the bed, and if you will condescend augustly to arrange your honourable body on anything so unworthy, Okamisan (the sweet little wife) will be bewildered with the honour.

"She tells you so in a sweet voice as she kneels and presses her face down against the backs of her tiny hands on the tatami before you. You protest that the honour is with you; that it is indescribably rude of you to venture to think of polluting so magnificent a futon. Then, with a low bow, you stretch yourself out upon it. Okamisan covers you with another futon, and doubling up again, lisps: 'Oyasumi nasai' ('Condescend to enjoy honourable tranquillity'). Mine host says the weather impresses him as being such as to encourage nap-taking also, and soon he is on another futon lying peacefully beside you, to be called when the bath is ready, for if it is afternoon all Japan takes a nap and afterwards a dip in the 'furo,' or wooden bath-tub, and has a rub down by a maid.

"Supposing you to be a foreigner who has just

arrived, and therefore a 'griffin,' in Yokohama slang, your first night in Japan is likely to be a new experience, especially if you are unfamiliar with the Far East. You may very well begin right here in Tokio, the capital of the Empire.

"You leave your shoes outside the door on entering, for the delicate texture of the bamboo matting, which is the upper surface of the tatami, would be torn by boot heels. If your feet are chilled, you may wear heelless slippers, but the native way is the best; that is, to go barefoot—a good preventive against colds and rheumatism. If you like, you may wear 'tabi.' Tabi are the native socks. They come just to the ankle, around which they fasten with hooks, and are like mittens in shape, having separate pockets for the great toes, just as mittens have for the thumbs. Tabi are convenient, because when wearing them your feet fit into the "zori" (sandals) and "geta" (wooden clogs), which the Japanese wear out of doors instead of shoes, and you may amble round as you please without the bother of bending over to lace or to button or to pull on a pair of boots. The slit in the tabi between the pocket for the great toe and the pocket for the other toes is to admit the thong by which the geta and zori are held to the foot.

"When your shoes are on one of the shelves in the stand, where you would look for a hat-rack in England, a maid will take you directly to your room along with your luggage, for there is no office in which to stop to register. There you will find little in the way of ornament, and no furniture at all. If you like you may have some brought in. There may be a 'kakemono' hanging in the alcove, and a 'gaku' over one of the cross-beams that hold the upper groove for the 'karakimi,' or sliding paper doors. The gaku is by a famous chirographer, and bears his seal. Likely enough the sentence is a maxim of Confucius.

"As there are no chairs, you will be glad that the Japanese floors are not like ours, and that the tatami are really soft. You will have 'zabuton,' or small square futon-like chair-cushions to sit on, and you will wish you had the chair, too. You will soon wonder what to do with your legs and feet, which you will discover can be very troublesome appendages. If only you could hang them over somewhere, or even down a hole. But there is no suitable hole. If you wish a table to use in writing down your 'first impressions,' after the manner of most griffins, the maid will bring you one a foot high, which you may grow used to if you persevere; but then you will not be a griffin—you will have been graduated.

"If it is toward the end of an afternoon, you should have a bath. You will find it amusing, refreshing, and possibly embarrassing. When the maid has scrubbed your back, it will be time for 'ban meshi,' or evening meal. You will find the chopsticks unexpectedly easy to manage. Soon after this, as you are tired, you are ready for the bed to come to you.

"As you are not used to sleeping on the floor yet, even a soft one, you had better order 'futon ni mai,' or, if you are tender, 'sam mai.' ('Ni' means 'two,' and 'san' or 'sam' means 'three.' 'Mai' is an auxiliary numeral used when counting flat things.) You clap your hands instead of pressing the button of an electric bell, and from far back in the interior of the house comes a drawn out 'Hai-i-i-i, tadaima.' 'Hai' is only a signal cry, meaning that the maid hears you. It does not mean 'yes.' 'Tadaima,' the dictionaries say, means 'now,' 'just now,' 'at present,' or 'presently.' In some tea-houses you will find it is the equivalent of the Spanish word 'manana.' Tokio maids are quick, however, and in a moment the karakimi slide to one side, and a little body is kneeling just beyond awaiting orders.

"You say you are sleepy and would like a nap, and you ask for an extra futon. 'Hai, kashikomari mashita,' replies the bright-eyed maiden as she bends low. Then with a 'go men nasai' she pushes the karakimi wide open, and calls out, 'Ne san, chotto oide. Sensei ne masu desu yo!' ('Elder sister, come here a moment. The Learned One would sleep!')

"Elder sister, who, by the way, is as likely to be the younger of the two, comes along the verandah from the kitchen, her bare feet sounding patty-pat on the polished wood. She goes to the wall and slides open the door of the 'fukuro dana,' or cupboard, which you thought was the entrance to another room. There are the futon folded up on a horizontal shelf, which divides the cupboard so that it looks like the two berths of a stateroom on board ship.

"'Ni mai desu ne, dana san?' she says. ('You want two pieces, don't you, master?') And then with the

THE OBEDIENT BED

THE OBEDIENT BED

sweetest little smile, and with her head a bit to one side like a bird, she asks : ' Makura fu futatsu, desuka ?' ' Makura ' is pillow, and she asks if you wish two.

"The futon are spread out one upon the other, and a sheet perhaps is laid on top. Sheets, however, are new to Japan. Then comes the big 'yagu,' or top futon, which is longer than the others, and has sleeves like a huge kimono. This is bunched up at the foot of the bed, ready to be pulled over you when you have laid down.

"The small object at the head of your bed, which looks like a cigar-box on edge surmounted by a roll of paper, is the 'makura.' No one need envy your first night's experience with it. You will discover that your head is as heavy as though it were solid lead, and, therefore—which is all the comfort you'll have out of the sensation—that it cannot possibly be empty. You will likely dream of being beheaded or unheaded, and of falling over the brinks of precipice after precipice.

"In the morning your head will be stationary, for the hinges of your neck will be too rusty to turn even a little bit. It will take time to master the makura, but you will like it when you are used to it. If you will examine closely you will see that it is not a cigar-box, but a truncated pyramid, four or five inches high, hollow, with a rectangular base and a groove on top, in which lies a slender cushion stuffed with bran. Upon this cushion ne san binds a few layers of paper, which are changed every morning.

"There is a drawer at one end of the makura, in which you will find tobacco, extremely fine cut and of attenuated flavour. You may take 'ippuku' (one puff), as the Japanese say, with small danger of nervous prostration. There may be one or two 'kiseru,' or pipes, in the drawer. If not, surely there are several on the tray beside the 'tabako ban,' the square little rosewood box with the earthenware 'hibachi,' or brazier, in it, and the 'haifuki,' as the bamboo tube is called, which is a combination of ash-receiver and cuspidor. Bits of burning charcoal are in the hibachi for lighting your pipe. The haifuki is for ashes, burnt matches, and the other uses of a cuspidor.

"If it is not too late in the season, you will need a 'kaya,' or mosquito net. Ne san will have it unfolded and hung up by cords at its four corners in almost no time. It is always green, and usually has red bindings. When you are inside you will be well shut off from the evening breezes as well as from the mosquitoes, and will not feel the need of the 'yagu' or upper futon.

"You have watched these proceedings with amusement, and now that everything seems ready you wonder why the 'elder sisters' do not patter back to the kitchen. But all is not ready. They must take away the 'rosoku,' or paper-wicked candles, or the 'rampu'—as the Japanese pronounce lamp—and put the night lantern, the 'andon,' in its place. This is a large square white paper affair, standing on a frame a couple of feet above the 'tatami,' and lighted by a taper that juts out over the edge of a small saucer of oil of sesame within.

"While you are waiting and wondering, they are

doing the same thing. They will bring the night lamp as soon as you are safely under the kaya.

"'Why doesn't honourable master undress?' they are thinking, and you, 'Why the deuce don't those maids go?' A Japanese friend explains to you, perhaps, and you get him between you and them, and, partially disrobing, slip under the kaya. Then he explains your trepidation to the ne san, and all three have a great laugh at your shyness.

"Should you wish to go out to look at the moon or to study the weather probabilities for the morrow, or the 'asago,' which is Japanese for morning glory, before retiring, ne san accompanies you and stands patiently by, humming an old love tune. She has a dipper at the 'chosubachi,' and will pour water for you to wash your hands, and will offer you a brand new 'tenui' after your ablutions, on which to dry yourself. Ne san is not an imaginative person. She guides you as a matter of course, and takes good care of you. She sees you safely in bed, and doubling up into a little bunch, she says most humbly: 'Oyasumi nasai.' Then sh-sh-sh-click, the karakimi are pushed together, and you are in bed in Japan. You'll rather like it after a month's experience.

"You will not find bedrooms in Japanese houses. But wherever you go you will find futon are plentiful, and wherever there is space for one, there you may have a bed. The servants—men, women, boys, and girls—sleep on the kitchen floor, or, more often, on the floor of the room opening into the kitchen, in a long row, depending on the size of the room and the number of servants.

"In a first-class tea-house or hotel, if you look in early of a morning, you will find several rows of futon reaching quite across the main room, each with a head hanging out comfortably over the top of one of those hollow wooden pillows. To the Japanese they are rather neck-rests than head-rests, but to the foreign mind the word rest is not applicable to makura. Except in the case of young children, no two people are on the same futon.

"Using futon and the floor instead of bedsteads is a great saving of house space, and is convenient in many other ways. The futon are easily aired, and may be carried about readily when moving. In case of fire they are quickly packed up and put out of danger. They are cheap, too, except those used by the rich, which are filled with pure silk wadding and covered with heavy, heavy silk. Even then they cost less than hair mattresses in England.

"As much of the exterior as well as of the interior walls of Japanese houses are sliding doors, which grow loose and wobbly with the changing of the seasons, from wet to dry and then to wet again; and with the shaking of the five hundred earthquakes that occur each year, there is no lack of chinks and crevices which, however admirable for ventilation, are rather too cooling in winter. It behoves you to have heat if you would be comfortable. The Japanese have neither open fireplaces nor stoves. They make no attempt to heat their houses, but they try to keep their toes and fingers warm by means of a 'kotatsu'—that is a square hibachi, sunk in the floor and having a wooden frame above it.

THE OBEDIENT BED

This supports the futon that are laid over it and prevents their catching fire. There is a grating, too, just over the fire, something like a grill iron.

"In winter the beds are arranged round the kotatsu, and consequently for the first half of the night your feet are in an oven, but as morning approaches, and the charcoal fire dwindles, the oven changes and is more like an ice-box.

"When you give a party to your friends, and, the wee sma' hours approaching, you would fain retire, do not hesitate to do so, but do not hint anything thereof to your guests. That would be a sad breach of etiquette. They own the house while they are there and all that is therein. Your course is quietly to disappear to the remotest apartment you have and call the bed to come to you. It is good form to do this, for it allows the merriment to continue unrestrained. Should anyone ask for you, the maids will say that you are just outside, and will be in 'tadaima'—a safe term to use. In the morning, if your saké was good, you will find your friends sleeping sweetly on your spare futon, a bed having gone to each of them by the courtesy of ne san."

CHAPTER VIII

ONE WHO WON

WHILE in Tokio this trip, we were onlookers at a poker game once, as guests of a man of rank. Though we did not take a hand, we had a worthy night of it. The game was of a magnitude we had never seen before—and in such simple yet exquisite surroundings: a glorious place for the purpose, or for any other purpose! Our friends were of some distinction, too, and most interesting in their native manner.

"Hitotsu, futatsu, mitsu, yotsu, itsutsu—aka bakari" (One, two, three, four, five—red only), said Prince Sakusama, at the end of the first jack-pot, as he counted a straight flush, beginning with the ace of hearts, and laid it on the low ebony table in one of the famous tea-houses on Sumida Gawa.

"I win?" he asked, as he paused a moment and looked round at his companions. Then, with a gentle inclination to those round the table, "Aragato de gozaimasu" ("The chips and Peach Blossom, too. Shall I put her in the kitty?").

"If your Highness did so," said a young Baron who had just returned with an Embassy from

London, "all of us would play to lose, for as your Highness has deigned to declare the rules of the game, give the kitty to the player who is hit the hardest. To play poker to lose would be to debauch its pristine purity."

"We must never do that, Baron, surely. Let us play a round of jacks."

He clapped his hands, and from the far interior of the tea-house, beyond many partitions of paper sliding-doors, an answering, "Hai tadaima," long drawn, soft and musical, floated in, telling the prince that his summons had been heard. A moment later and the paper doors at the end of the room slid noiselessly in their grooves and disclosed a bundle of daintiness on the tatami just outside.

It was Peach Blossom, kneeling low, with her face almost touching the soft bamboo matting, and her tiny hands pressed palm down together just before her.

She besought His Highness to deign to pardon her audacious effrontery in responding to the august summons, and begged that if he would condescend to command so unworthy a piece of stupid mud as she, he would deign to consider her ready to receive the augustly honourable orders.

"Saké," said the Prince, and as Momo-no-Hana closed the sliding door and pattered away for the hot rice-beer, His Highness tore the cover from a fresh pack of cards and began to shuffle them. The Baron cut and the game proceeded.

Five better poker faces were never gathered about a table. There was not a sign of nerves in any one of them. Each player skinned his hand and decided whether to draw or pass or to stand pat, but never a sign of his thoughts was given in his countenance. Each had the expression of a doorknob. Good hands and bad hands come to a doorknob, but one can tell nothing of them by looking at it.

These five men in the tea-house on the bank of the Sumida Gawa, which flows through the heart of Tokio, bore some of the best-known names in the Japanese Empire. Three of them had been "Daimiyo" and had owned provinces as absolutely as anything may be owned in this world. Their revenues had been counted by the 100,000 "koku."[1] They had lived in royal state, each with his castles and his army and board of councillors.

But Commodore Perry had changed all that, and now these men were living in the capital with one-tenth of their former incomes, but with no one to support or worry about, outside their personal households.

Of the other two, his Highness, Prince Sakusama, was of the Shogun's family, which had ruled the empire until the restoration in 1868, and the other was of the samurai class. His fathers had been fighting-men for full two thousand years, as his family records showed. He had studied abroad, was a graduate of Harvard, an M.A. of Oxford, and a Ph.D. of Heidelberg. It was said that he had carved his name on the face of a German student who had been so unlucky as to challenge him. He was a vice-minister now, and had married the daughter of

[1] A koku is about five bushels (of rice).

ONE WHO WON

a merchant with much money. (Before 1871 he would have been sentenced to "hara-kiri" for *mésalliance.*) All five had learned to play abroad. They had been together in a Japanese club in London, the presiding genius of which was their Consul-General, who knew the great American game as well as did ever a Kentucky colonel.

Now that they were at home again, they were only too willing to meet wherever a chance afforded, and the tea-house of the Rising Moon knew them well. Its mistress was glad to see them, for the players and their friends were a hungry and thirsty lot, and did not spare the kitty, out of which the chief loser had to pay all expenses.

The round of jacks was under way when Momo-no-Hana came in with the saké. When saké is ordered in a tea-house, food is served with it, for the host knows well the evil effects of drinking on an empty stomach, and besides there is profit in comestibles. So Omomo San was followed by a procession of similar blossoms, each with a dainty morsel on china dishes and lacquered trays. All these bearers of nectar and ambrosia were geisha, and indentured to masters of various geisha houses. Rumour had it that for certain sums of money, doubtless much exaggerated, the indenture papers of the more bewitching of these geisha had changed hands, so that the sweet singers were come under the guardianship of men of noble birth, who in the olden days could have cut in two the master of a geisha house and would have been accountable to no one. Food and drink disappeared rapidly, and then the game went on, while music and singing kept accompaniment. Finally came the last jackpot of the last round. It bore out the rumour as to the transference of indenture papers,[1] for when the last call was made and his Highness had reckoned up the contents, he found Cherry Bud, Chrysanthemum, and Plum Blossom were added to his list, besides Little Posy and One Thousand Joys. He had won the whole procession. Each player laughed as though he might have been himself the principal winner, exchanged saké cups with all the others, and planned to meet again.

Looking out over the slow Sumida, and watching the house-boats with their gay paper lanterns as the sendo poled them along the shores in the light of the rising moon, Sakusama dipped his saké cup in the basin, and handing it to him who had lost just too little to be entitled to the kitty, said—

"Kono tsugi goshiawase! Dozo ippai onomu nasai." Which means, being literally interpreted, "Next time your honourable luck good probably will be. Graciously condescend a cupful of saké to imbibe."

[1] Buying indenture papers was not equivalent to buying the geisha. To buy her was to buy her release from her master. That was all. She was not bound, legally, to serve the buyer. From her point of view it might be the honourable thing to do, however.

CHAPTER IX

THINKING IN JAPANESE

WHAT wonders a little word will work! It was the mellifluous "tadaima," for instance, our old friend of the inns and the tea-houses, that set Gardner and me at the language. It had followed us on our trip to Tokio, and at the time that it "set" us it had been floating in from Okashi's yashiki for quite two hours.

Something had happened to the "fire-box" that our cook had contrived for the viands we needed on our feast days, so we were waiting for our dinner. We were hungry, we were in a hurry, and the hour was late, yet no matter how much we clapped our hands all we elicited was "tadaima"—tadaima instead of sustenance! Every four minutes of the two hours either Gardner or I had called until the fingers of our right hands had raised welts on our left hands' palms, and further "popping" was painful.

We were "na sae ticklit," as a Drumtochty man might have said, over the monotony of the responses to our summons, but it was Sunday and we did not speak out what we thought. I had found out something about "tadaima" the first night I was in Tokio, and I had described my impressions to Gardner. We both knew that in the dictionaries it was opposite the word "immediately." Whoever juxtaposed it there may have fancied for the moment that he was at work on a list of antonyms. One could not well imagine a word more opposite to "immediately" than "tadaima." Its location in the dictionary was a good one from the antonymic point of view.

"I'll tell you what we'll have to do, Partner," said my good friend, as he clapped his hands for the fifteenth time, rather mildly, and listened to the thirtieth "tadaima."

"Is it far?" I asked. I thought he was about to suggest a tea-house.

"No, I don't mean to go anywhere," he replied. "I was about to observe that we must study the language. This eternal tadaima disturbs the equanimity I would maintain. My soul protests. So does my appetite department. If we had learned Japanese we should not be sitting here like a couple of blind claqueurs, we should have proceeded to the kitchen at the first indication of delay and have remonstrated so accurately, so precisely, and so emphatically, that by this time we should have been within sound of the surf at Sakaiko." Sakaiko is a grand place for surf some days, and Gardner and I went there often, but to-day we should be late.

Yes, Gardner was right. If we had taken up the language we should have been more comfortable internally. Tadaima would be a lesson to us.

"True," I replied. "We must learn the lingo"; and straightway we began. There was no "tadaima"

THINKING IN JAPANESE

about Gardner once his mind had determined itself. Kojiki San had various books which he said kind lady missionaries had loaned to him once at a Christian school in Kanazawa. While Gardner went over for them I made some tea. Then we began. The book we first read was by an Englishman who held a unique position, considering his nationality. He was Professor of Japanese in the Imperial University of Japan, in Tokio. We also had articles by Captain Brinkley, R.A., editor of the *Japan Mail*, whose particular information about Japan, and general information about everything, filled us with enthusiastic awe; by Percival Lowell, who would have us believe the Japanese have no souls; by Lafcadio Hearn, who knows that Japanese souls are as plentiful as any people's, though not always encumbered with material bodies, and he has written about them with such rare illumination that others may see as he does. The more illusive the object towards which Mr. Hearn's mind turns attention, the more brilliantly he seizes it and presents it to his readers.

His books, however, were not among those the missionary loaned to Kojiki. Mr. Hearn does not approve the missionary, and says so frankly. We had, besides, an Etymology by Imbrie, which gave us opportunity for learning by practical examples the uses of particular words; and dear old Hepburn's Dictionary, in sombre black, the result of many years unselfish labour by a Christian missionary who was also a scholar and a physician. But the books that helped us most were by the Englishman at the University, Basil Hall Chamberlain. His *Colloquial*

Japanese, Things Japanese, and *Handbook of Japan* (in which Mr. Mason collaborated) were a joy—and are so even to this day. May his shadow never grow less!

We found out a lot of things about Japanese that very afternoon, things that everyone else knew probably, but which we had not happened to think about—to wit, Japanese is not even second cousin to Chinese, though in the matter of loans Chinese has been a good uncle. Japanese is an only child, and its parentage, though certainly respectable, is doubtful. It has a cousin in the Luchu Islands, and remote kindred possibly in Corea, where there is some anatomical resemblance. Gardner's sympathetic heart was touched by this apparent isolation, and he declared he would look into the matter to see if he could not find relatives among the Manchus or the Mongols.

We had thought to learn to write Japanese, but, after a cursory survey of the ground we must needs go over, we decided to devote ourselves at first to speaking. The written language would take time— ten years, perhaps, if we kept steadily at it twenty-four hours a day as I reckoned it, though Gardner was inclined to say twenty-six, and we felt it would be hardly wise to write much at first. We could not have begun at the beginning anyway—not the kind of beginning that other languages begin at, for there is no alphabet in Japanese. We should have had to learn sets of syllables instead of letters. There are two of these, and six ways of writing the one more generally in use. Then there would be four thousand ideographs to commit to memory (a number said to be sufficient for reading the daily paper comfortably), which the Japanese write in two different styles, cursive and standard, as the spirit moves them, and in various other ways if they happen to be men of learning. These ideographs, Professor Chamberlain assured us, had three or four different readings, according to context. Then in the next paragraph, to give zest to his description, he declared that a printed page was likely enough to have all the different forms of the characters scattered over it pell-mell. Perhaps Gardner was correct in saying "twenty-six."

With the spoken language there was hope. In the first place it was agglutinative. A language that glues on its case endings, and builds up its grammatical forms of speech with little pellets of cement, cannot but be hedonic. Ever since we were children we had looked forward to having an agglutinative language right down where we could study it without getting hurt. Now we had one. Then, too, to go back to my early days, I recalled the cloud grammar had cast over my young life—how my soul had protested against it, and how it had come round at ten o'clock each school day as though my soul had never spoken, or as though I had no soul (I knew grammar had none). It was with gratitude to Professor Chamberlain, therefore, that I read this paragraph of his.

"A word as to the parts of speech in Japanese. Strictly speaking, there are but two, the verb and the noun." ("The only parts I ever knew!" I purred.)

"The particles or 'post positions' and suffixes, which take the place of our prepositions, conjunctions, and conjunctional terminations, were themselves originally fragments of nouns and verbs. The pronoun and numeral are simply nouns. The true adjective (including the adverb) is a sort of neuter verb. But many words answering to our adjectives and adverbs are nouns in Japanese. There is no article. Altogether our grammatical categories do not fit the Japanese language well."

Another interesting feature was the honorific. That was a delight second only to the absence of parts of speech. In Japanese it seems all one's own things are mean and vile, while the other fellow's are honourable, august, divine. Gardner and I practised this, and soon each had the other on a throne while he himself grovelled before him most abjectly. We learned to apologise for living, and to say, "Yesterday I had the honour of being rude to you," or, "To-morrow will your augustness condescend to remind decayed me to buy some honourable tea?" etc.

If I wished to look at the laundry marks on Gardner's collars, to see if the august washerwoman was not a thief, I should say: "May I turn towards your honourable collars my adoring glance?" but if I wished Gardner to look at something of mine, I should say: "O Gardner, Prince, august glance deign towards my meretricious cake of Persian healing pine-tar soap," or whatever it was.

It so happened that our kimono were quite alike, it having been necessary to buy three pieces of silk to make two robes—one piece, according to the new police regulations, not being sufficient to clothe a foreigner. Often we mixed these up, and in trying to explain in Japanese (English being taboo out of school hours) we had some difficulty in establishing which was whose, and our honorifics got into a mess. For the life of me I could not say whether the robe in my hand was Gardner's august mantle or my unmentionable rags. Gardner would be in equal mystery as to what he held. Then he would deliver himself as to the august forgetfulness of the honourable idiot that had disarranged the room that morning under the pretence of sweeping up, and would say: "Well, let's wear them as they are. Your heavenly attire may now have become by my possession even as that righteousness which has not faith. Who knows? Let us label them somewhere inside the sleeve where the mark won't show."

Having settled this we started in on a few sentences, our daily commitment. Below are some samples I give on Professor Chamberlain's authority. In the first line are the Japanese words, which flow easily as Italian, and with as little emphasis on syllables as there is in French. Then comes the interlinear translation. In the third line is the free English translation, which shows how the idea hidden in the Japanese sentence looks when it appears in English. Not only is the second line literal, but it represents, as accurately as English words can, the order and sequence of the ideas as they exist in the Japanese mind. After this transcript of a native thought, it is not impossible to believe that globe-trotting book writers sometimes fall short of perfect comprehension when they describe the workings of the Far Eastern mind. That the Japanese think differently from the Europeans is evident enough. Their mental machinery is of another kind — the product of a different factory — and put together on different principles of construction. An occurrence that suggests a certain train of thought to the European suggests a totally different train of thought to the Japanese. His whole intellectual inheritance is different, as well as his personal experience, his environment during childhood, and the habits of the society of which he has been a member. His ideals spring from a different source, and his point of view is vastly different. As one instance of this, the absence of the words "you" and "I" are illustrative. He has no real pronouns in his language, but when he would present the idea of "you" he says "honourable side"— the idea being that the side of the room at which you sit is the place of honour, while he is humbly at your feet. If he would say "I" he uses the word "watakushi" (pronounced wa-ta-k-shi), which means selfishness.

A study of the interlinear translations is the only way to get at the "Japanese mode." Here are some specimens :—

O   ki no doku   Sama.
Honourable poison-of-the-spirit Mr.

I am sorry for your sake.

Go   burei   moshi-agemashita.
August   rudeness (I)   said-lifted.

I was very rude to you.

Kiite   itadakite   gozaimasu
Hearing   wishing-to-put-on-the-head   am

I wish you would be so kind as to ask.

O shiete   itadakitai
Teaching   wish-to-put-on-the-head

I wish you would be so kind as to show me how.

We said these over and over on all occasions, and even invented occasions particularly for their use. We became so polite that we found it difficult to speak truthfully, and if we had not known each other so well we should indeed have become suspicious.

One day as I returned from a conversation class of young Buddhists not far away, I heard Gardner recite as follows. I have it exactly, for I copied it from the text-book he was studying:—

"No, indeed! having risen hands wash act even forthcomes not was. Washing basin's water altogether freeze-sticking having finished how doing even doing way is not was." My heart beat with joy. At last he had learned to think in Japanese. Should anyone be sceptical as to Gardner's accuracy, let him look in Chamberlain's *Colloquial Japanese*,

p. 263, the second example on the page. Here it is:—

    Iya, mo! okite te wo arau
    No indeed having-risen hands (accusative particle) wash

    koto mo dekimasen deshita
    act even forth comes not was

    Chozu bachi no mizu ga
    Washing basin (possessive particle 's) water (nominative particle)

    maru de kori-tsuite shimatte
    altogether freeze-sticking having-finished

    do shite mo shiyo ga
    how doing even doing-way (nominative particle)

    arimasen deshita
    is-not was

And this is the translation:—

"No, indeed! When I got up, I couldn't wash my hands. The basin was entirely frozen over, and all my efforts to break the ice were in vain."

CHAPTER X

BO CHAN

WE had not been with Okashi long before we had made friends with the babies of the immediate neighbourhood—more than two dozen of them all told. Like other bachelors, we were authorities on infants. Our knowledge helped us with the west coast youngsters.

I am sure that it is true to-day as it was forty years ago, when Sir Rutherford Alcock wrote: " And this, I should say, is the very paradise of babies." Sir Rutherford saw innumerable infants in the three years he was in Japan, and as he was a physician as well as a diplomat, and a keen observer, as all physicians and diplomats should be, we may take it that he spoke the truth. Judging by his descriptions of the native youngsters it is small wonder that Her Majesty's Minister to the Court of the " Great Prince," or Tycoon, as the Shogun called himself in those days, had to write about them. He could not help it. His book, by the way, *The Capital of the Tycoon*, is a vivid and delightful picture of the days when Old Japan was passing away and New Japan was nearly ready to come out of its chrysalis.

Japanese babies of the twentieth century are as irresistible as they were when Sir Rutherford played with them. They are precocious, too, for they are a year old the moment they are born, and two years old the first New Year's Day. That is the way the Japanese reckon age; counting the year in which the baby is born "one," the next year "two," and so on. If you had been born in Japan just as the temple bell was about to strike twelve the night of December 31, you would be, according to the Japanese mind, two years old with the first clang. So in Japan, which to Europeans and Americans is a very strange country indeed, one of a pair of twins might be a year older than the other.

Some travellers to this wonderful Empire have said that Japanese babies never cry. That is not quite true. They have all the apparatus necessary—midriff, lungs, and vocal cords in excellent condition, and they know how to use these with effect; but nevertheless one sees fewer tears in the Land of the Rising Sun, and hears less wailing, than in other countries. This surprises the visitor, for he notes the throngs of children in the streets—the playground for almost all the youngsters in Japan; he sees them tumble about so on their rather awkward wooden clogs, falling often with a good hard "splap" upon the roadway, that he wonders at hearing only shouts of glee and laughter. The children bounce about as harmlessly as rubber balls. Often when a youngster stumbles and goes down with force enough almost to dent the pavement, the stranger looking on is sure there will be weeping. But the child is up again quickly; there is the little pause which children at home use in gathering all their energy for a great boo-hoo! (the stranger knows it is coming and wonders what it will sound like in Japanese); then, having recalled what it was thinking about at the instant it fell, the youngster scampers on as merrily as before. The fall had interrupted its train of thought for the moment, that was all.

Because the children play all over the streets, one needs a "betto" when one goes out for a drive in Japan. A betto is a footman—a most appropriate word—whose business it is to run on ahead of the horse to clear the way. He does not lack for exercise, for his arms and legs are busy from the time the drive begins until it is over. Japanese children are not too careful, and their mothers do not use nearly as many safeguards as do the women of Western countries, but there are fewer accidents. This is rather a mystery, for every Japanese house has an "engawa," or porch, and these porches do not have fences along the edge to keep the infants from falling off, nor are there gates at the tops of stairways, when the houses happen to have stairways, yet I never saw a Japanese child fall downstairs nor off a porch, nor ever heard of anyone else witnessing such a mishap.

Another thing about these youngsters is that they are all little gentlemen and ladies—merry and happy as possible, but not rough. Mrs. Chaplin-Ayrton says this trait may be more apparent than real, for a grown person judges of the roughness of children's play by the number of things they break, and in a

Japanese house there is no furniture or bric-a-brac to destroy—not even chairs, for the natives sit on the floor. On the other hand, Professor Chamberlain lays this gentleness to less robust health, which means less animal spirits than foreign children have.

However this may be, the health officers say that the deathrate for children is lower in Japan than it is in Europe and in America. This is as it should be, in a country where the houses are off the ground a foot or two and have no cellars, and the air inside is as fresh as it is out, where, too, in such places at least as Tokio, everyone bathes and has a good scrubbing every day. From 800,000 to 1,000,000 persons go to the public baths of the capital daily, and there are tens of thousands of private baths besides. That is a good showing for a city with a population of two millions.

When an infant is seven days old, its mother displays her talent as a barber by shaving its head all but a little bit at the back of the neck right at the base of the skull, like a goatee that had strayed from its proper place. Later on she experiments with various designs to discover the most becoming. Sometimes she shaves the top and the rim, and leaves a tonsure; sometimes she leaves only the rim; sometimes a scalp-lock and two love-locks only, but always she is picturesque. This decorative shaving process continues until the youngster goes to school, say, when he or she is five or six. Then, usually, the mother also weans him.

A disagreeable result often attends this shaving among the children of the lower classes; not serious at all, but offensive to the sight. It is eczema. Heads are sometimes white with it. The only thing necessary for its disappearance is soap and water, but in this one case Japanese superstition says "no" to soap and water. Poverty and superstition are often hand in hand, and the Japanese poor have many superstitions. They believe the cause of the eczema is the ill health in their children working through the scalp, an outward and visible sign of an inward and physical wickedness. This physical wickedness they wish their children to be rid of, so they encourage eczema. They wash the youngsters faces and bodies daily, but omit the shampoo. Professor Chamberlain calls attention to the fact, anent Japanese "topsy-turvydom," that young subjects of the Mikado stop shaving when they begin to go to school instead of beginning to shave when they leave off going to school.

After what has been said about the Japanese way of reckoning age it may seem strange they should have birthday celebrations, or else one might think it would be consistent with the native custom for everyone to celebrate his or her birthday on January 1. There is a grand national birthday then, that lasts two weeks; but apart from this there are two more birthday celebrations—one on the third day of the third month (March 3) for all the girls in Japan, and the other on the fifth day of the fifth month (May 5) for all the boys.

The girls celebrate with a festival of dolls. At that time Japan, which in many ways suggests a land of dolls to the European, is "dollier" than ever.

The dolls are of all kinds and sizes, and often wonderfully life-like, so that at first glance one is not sure whether a girl is playing with a real baby or a make-believe. Japanese girls carry their dolls about on their backs snugly tucked away inside their jackets, just as Japanese nurses carry babies. And, oddly enough, nurses in Japan are often not much older than the babies they are caring for. Sometimes one sees a little nurse playing hopscotch while a baby is fast asleep on her back, its tiny head rolling about this way and that, and its face looking right up at the sun, so that were it not for the protection of its thick eyelids the glare would make it blind.

The boys have a grand time of it, too, when their turn comes. Then the air is full of fishes, as two months earlier the streets were full of dolls. The fishes are "koi," as the Japanese call them; scientific men say they are *Cyprinus hæmatopterus*, but they are much better looking than that, though fully as long. What they represent is large carp swimming bravely against the stream, as the parents hope their sons will do on reaching man's estate. The carp, which are attached to the tops of tall poles, are hollow, with wide-open mouths and paper bodies, through which the breezes blow, keeping them distended, and swaying to and fro in a movement similar to swimming. Every house where there are boys has these fishes up aloft, and many other carp down below, but of a kind that taste better than paper full of wind.

Hopscotch is by no means the only game Japanese boys and girls have in common with children in

JAPANESE NURSES CARRY BABIES ON THEIR BACK

other parts of the world. They have battledore and shuttlecock, archery, bouncing balls, tops, kites, prisoner's base, snow-man, snow-forts, puss-in-the-corner, fencing, peas-pudding hot, flower cards, and many forfeit games.

Their battledores are works of art. In shape they are something like a short paddle, but with square corners instead of round. The face is smooth polished wood, and the back ornamented with striking designs in relief, often portraits of famous actors or heroes of ancient times. The shuttlecock is the same sort of thing that children use in this country. Archery is popular, and many Japanese have great skill at it. Their bows are strong. When not strung, these appear to be wrong side out, so queerly are they bent. The archery rules are rather formal as to the position one should stand in, and irksome to the beginner unless he is an enthusiast. There is a sort of baby archery, too, for indoors, which is amusing. The bows are a foot and a half long, perhaps, and the arrows about twelve inches from notch to point.

Japanese girls and boys are as clever as jugglers with their bouncing balls. While keeping them going they play at posture dancing also, spinning round, clapping their hands, passing a fan over and under the ball, catching it on the backs of their hands and guiding it round the room or along the road at will. They would make pretty pictures for the cinematograph. Tops and kites are much the same as those commonly seen in this country. Youngsters have kite battles. They gum powdered glass to the strings and each tries to cut the other's kite free.

The Japanese have some wonderful tricks with tops, and the visitor should be sure to see the top juggler, who can send his top humming up one arm, across his shoulders, and down the other arm, on to the palm of his hand, or out on to the end of a fan, whence he will make it jump to the edge of a sword, where it will spin as comfortably as though it were on solid ground. He can also throw it so that it will return to him, boomerang fashion. He can also spin two tops together, one inside the other.

"Prisoner's base" is the same in this country, except that the officer is called "oni," which means demon, or ghost, or evil spirit. "Puss-in-the-corner" is an oni also. "Blind-man's buff" is quite the same, but if you play it with Japanese I may warn you not to say "come here," in English, to anyone you may be trying to catch. It will be all right to say in Japanese, "chotto oide" (come here a moment), or "oide nasai" (condescend to come here). The person spoken to will not "oide," of course, if he or she can help himself or herself, but if you called out in English, "Come here," as I know a foreigner did once, you may interrupt the game. Come here (in Japanese characters written "ka-mi") means foreign dog. "Inu" is the word for native dog, but the first foreigners in Yokohama, American and English folk, always said "come here" to their dogs, and the expression has become the native word for dogs not Japanese.

Stilts, as the children use them in Japan, would

not be comfortable for European children, unless they were accustomed to go barefoot, as all native children go. The long upright pole comes up between the big toe and the next toe to it, and the whole length of the foot rests on the round crosspiece, which sticks out like one arm of a cross. The foot really grasps the pole monkey fashion, for, being accustomed to clogs and the thongs that hold the clogs on, the Japanese foot is much more prehensile than the European foot.

Experts say that Japanese "Checkers," which the natives call "Go," is more difficult than our chess. All classes of society play it a great deal. Good players receive diplomas. There are grand national tournaments, and the championship brings great honour to the holder and to his house. It is said that one family has won this continuously for over one hundred years. "Shogi," or Japanese chess, is a difficult game, but so popular that even the coolies play it well.

Fencing is something that both men and women used to study in the days of the "samurai" (knights) and their two swords. It sounds much rougher than it really is, for the long two-handed bamboo sticks make a loud report whenever they strike.

The Japanese call our cards "Turampu" (trumps), and play them as we do, but they have a tiny set of their own which they call "Hana" (flowers) and deal round to the right instead of to the left as we deal. A good lot of the fun comes in with the scoring; sometimes the losers receive a black mark on the face with a brush for each point they lose. The winners give them these marks on the face with India ink. At the end of an evening's playing the players look not unlike tatooed savages.

The game of "Jack-stones" or "Knuckle-bones" is common all over the country, but the children use small bags instead of knuckle-bones, for Japan is not a mutton country. Sheep do not thrive, because they have a habit of eating bamboo grass, which spoils both their wool and the meat.

The game of "Kitsune" (Fox), is famous for the quickness it demands. To play it, make a slip noose in the middle of a length of rope. Two players take hold of this rope, one at each end, and hold it as nearly taut as they can without closing the noose. The noose is the trap. A third player, the fox, sits half-way between them, facing the noose. Just opposite to him, on the other side of the noose, is a cup or a cake, which is the prize. The fox's object is to reach through the noose, grab the prize and pull it back through the noose before the two players holding the rope can catch him in the trap. If they catch him he pays a forfeit, if they do not he takes the cake.

Another game "Hana, hana" (Nose, nose), has something of the same idea in it as "Simon says 'thumbs up.'" Sight controls action more effectively than sound, and in "Hana, hana" the leader takes advantage of this by ordering one thing while doing another. The other players are apt to follow the motions rather than the commands. For instance, the girl (or boy) at the head, tips his nose with his first finger, saying "Nose, nose, nose, eye!" at the

THE GAME OF "KITSUNE" FOX

same time putting his finger to his chin. The others who must be looking into the leader's face, will find their fingers on their chins too, unless they are alert. They should have touched their eyes in obedience to the command "eyes," if they would not receive an ink spot or pay some other forfeit.

Still another "Hana" game is with a lot of loops of string, and is perhaps as amusing to children as any game can be. The loops must be made to order, one for each player, and must fit tightly round behind the ear and over the tip of the nose. If it is well on, and the player's nose is not too retroussé, the loop should not fall off without considerable effort on the player's part, especially as he or she may use the face muscles only. Other things being equal, the best face-maker wins.

Something similar to bobbing for apples is a game that even grandfathers play along with their grandchildren in Japan. It is easy there, because Japanese floors are covered with thick soft mats. Hard floors would not do, for a part of the game is that the players must walk on their knees. They hold their feet up behind them, one in each hand, and toddle forward to the centre of the room, where a fruit or a cake or a biscuit hang from the ceiling by a string. The idea is to bite out a piece, but biting and balancing are difficult to do simultaneously. Hence the fun.

"Kitsune ken" is a forfeit game for two or for any number of players. The players use signs for "kitsune" (fox), "teppo" (gun), and "otoko" (man). The idea of the game is that the man is mightier than the gun, the gun more deadly than the fox, and the fox more cunning than the man. Hands on the thighs or hips is the sign for "otoko"; one hand at the side and the other higher, and in front of the body, as though aiming a gun, is for "teppo"; while both hands up, one at each side of the head like a fox's ears, is "kitsune." The players sit facing each other, clap hands, or chant a line of a song; at the end of this each makes a sign. If both signs are alike there is no count, but if one makes the fox sign and the other the man sign, the man sign loses and has to submit to the forfeit. So the "man" sign wins over the "gun" sign, and the "gun" sign wins over the "fox" sign.

Exactly the same in principle is the forfeit game with one hand, where a closed fist represents a stone, an open palm a handkerchief, and the first and second fingers extended apart with the other two fingers and the thumb closed, represent scissors. Stone beats scissors, handkerchief beats stone, and scissors beat handkerchief.

Thumb wrestling is a common game, too. Players grasp hands with the thumbs sticking up, holding each other by the four fingers only. The wrestling is a battle of thumbs, each thumb trying to bend the other down forward and hold it there.

There are some hand-slapping tricks, too, but one would need a cinematograph to explain them clearly.

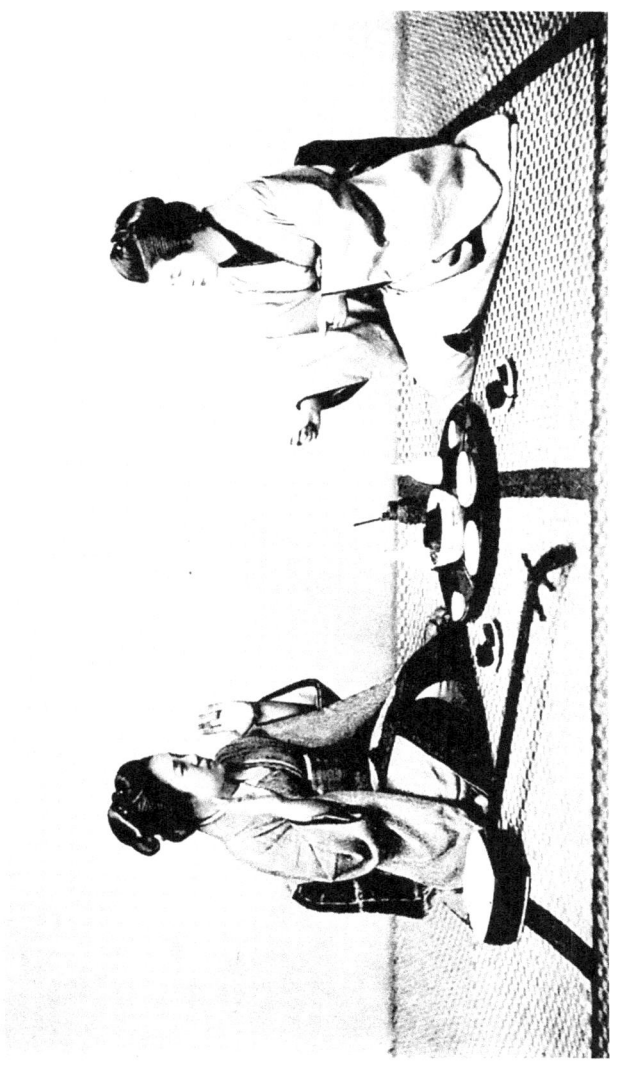

"KITSUNE KEN"

CHAPTER XI

O JO SAMA

ONE needs to see Japanese girls at home if one would know them, needs to live in the same household with them the year round, for there is much in their gentle lives they do not discover readily. We had a roomful in a class over in Okashi San's, and we saw much of the daughters of the families near by, but I suspect we never quite fathomed O Jo Sama. The glimpses travellers have in Tokio and in the seaport cities, where one sees native girls in the shops and the bazaars, in the restaurants, in the streets, round about the temple grounds, and in hundreds of the public schools, do not tell the story.

It is better to go into the country to those wonderfully picturesque and dainty homes along some old Kaido that the railways have not yet molested, where life to-day is the same that it was a thousand years ago. There one may see Japanese character as ages of feudalism moulded it and left it hardly a quarter of a century since, and may study the chief glory of this character—Japanese girls.

Japanese men do not know chivalry, as Westerners understand the word, but the womenfolk in two-score generations of repression are marvels of gentleness, discretion, and absolute unselfishness. A life that would be intolerable to an English or to an American girl is normal to the daughters of the Rising Sun, who meet its restrictions and encumbrances with tact, patience, and unending cheerfulness. How she can do so is difficult to understand, nor does seeing this perennial sunshine make the believing in it altogether easy. At first, though one may wonder and admire, and even reverence, the merry little body, one doubts there may be somewhat in her heart her looks belie. But on knowing her, as one sees her in the household daily through the year, one comes to believe that in the long line of her ancestors a process has been at work, with the result that those organs whose function is the display of irritation have become atrophied.

The opinion of Marion Crawford's sister, Mrs. Hugh Fraser, is worthy of attention. She was in Japan for years with her husband while he was Minister Plenipotentiary in Tokio. Mrs. Fraser says, "In real womanliness, which I take to mean a high combination of sense and sweetness, valour and humility, the Japanese lady ranks with any woman in the world, and passes before most of them."

One of these object lessons in the gentler virtues was Aya San, who lived not a great way from Tokio, the busy heart of the Empire; she was as jolly a youngster as one often sees even in Japan, and that is saying much. Though she lived so near the capital, she knew little of it. Household work and studies kept her too busy for sight-seeing. Her parents had come from near Kiyoto. They were of a southern class that had dispersed after the revolution of 1898. The father, who was a "samurai," that is of the military class, had the luck to receive a Government appointment in Tokio and then the luck to die. This left Aya San with her mother, her grandfather, and an infant brother, and a pension of four yen—about eight shillings—a month.

The income was not much for a family of gentlefolk to live on, but in those days when the daimiyo were discharging their retainers and handing their provinces over to the central Government, many a samurai household had less than that assured. It was different indeed compared to the days before the restoration, when the Shogun ruled and the Mikado was a sacred prisoner. Then the samurai had a large allowance from the rice-fields of his native province. My lord, the daimiyo, had seen to that. But now — threepence a day and four persons to live on it. However, they managed honourably one way or another, and so Aya's story is different from that of many a samurai's daughter.

Oka San, the mother, was of a sort one rarely sees in Tokio to-day, excepting on the stage, though in the country she is still in evidence. In a few years she will have disappeared entirely, for she is of the old order. Like the women of her time,

Oka San shaved her eyebrows when she left her own home to become a member of her husband's family, and had stained her teeth jet black. When she became a widow she cut her hair. Short hair, no eyebrows, and black teeth reads like a combination fatal to all attractiveness, nor are they agreeable to the unaccustomed eye. After a little, however, one ceases to remark them, and in the case of Oka San they did not destroy her charm, for her gentle kindliness of manner obliterated all thought of them.

Oji San, the grandfather, was an old man long in retirement—"inkiyo," as the Japanese say. His wants were simple. He spent his time at chess, and writing poetry and reading the Chinese classics. Aya San and Oka San had great reverence for him. They loved him doubtless, too, though in their tongue the word to use towards elders means to venerate. He it was who instructed them in "Onna Daigaku" ("The Whole Duty of Women," as Professor Chamberlain translates the title of the ancient treatise).[1] This was their gospel. Women of the West would have small patience with it, but Aya San and her mother believed it was very truth indeed. A man wrote it, of course, one Kaibara by name, who was a famous moralist.

Oji San used to read "The Whole Duty" to them, sitting on his cushion by the fire-box and arranging the charcoals now and then with the tiny fire-tongs, so that they would burn well and keep the water

[1] *Journal of the Royal Asiatic Society of Great Britain*, vol. x. p. iii.

in the small iron kettle hot for his fragrant cups of tea.

"Onna Daigaku" begins as follows, according to Professor Chamberlain's translation. One would think Kaibara was discoursing upon Hooligans rather than upon angels:—

"Seeing that it is the girl's destiny on reaching womanhood to go to a new home, and live in submission to her father-in-law, it is even more incumbent on her than it is on a boy to receive with all reverence her parents' instructions. Should her parents, through excess of tenderness, allow her to grow up self-willed, she will infallibly show herself capricious in her husband's house, and thus alienate his affection, while, if her father-in-law be a man of correct principles, the girl will find the yoke of these principles intolerable; she will hate and decry her father-in-law, and the end of these domestic dissensions will be her dismissal from her husband's house, and the covering of herself with ignominy. Her parents, forgetting the faulty education they gave her, may indeed lay all the blame on the father-in-law; but they will be in error; for the whole disaster should be rightly attributed to the faulty education the girl received from her parents.

"More precious in a woman is a virtuous heart than a face of beauty. The vicious woman's heart is ever excited; she glares wildly around her, she vents her anger on others, her words are harsh and her accents vulgar. When she speaks it is to set herself above others, to upbraid others, to envy others, to be puffed up with individual pride, to jeer at others, to outdo others,—all things at variance with the 'way' a woman should walk. The only qualities that befit a woman are gentle obedience, chastity, mercy, and quietness.

"From her earliest youth a girl should observe the line of demarcation separating women from men, and never, even for an instant, should she be allowed to see or hear the least impropriety. The customs of antiquity did not allow men and women to sit in the same apartment, to keep their wearing apparel in the same place, to bathe in the same place, or to transmit to each other anything from hand to hand. A woman going abroad at night must in all cases carry a lighted lamp, and (not to speak of strangers) she must observe a certain distance in her relations even with her husband and with her brethren. In our days, the women of the lower classes, ignoring all rules of this nature, behave themselves disorderly; they contaminate their reputation, bring down reproach on their parents and brethren, and spend their whole lives in an unprofitable manner. Is not this truly lamentable? It is written likewise in the 'Lesser Learning' that a woman must form no friendship and no intimacy except when ordered to do so by her parents or the 'middleman.' Even at the peril of her life must she harden her heart like rock or metal, and observe the rules of propriety."

So the "Onna Daigaku" goes on for many, many pages, which Oji San expounded, while Aya San and Oka San crouched before him on their shins, their tiny feet crossed under them, and their hands straight in front of them resting on their knees. They did not sit close by each other as mother and daughter might in this country. Personal contact is distasteful to Japanese. In their language there is no word that is the equivalent of the English word kiss, though Japanese dictionaries have borrowed the Chinese word "seppun." Aya San never kissed her mother, nor did Oka San ever kiss her child unless when Aya was a tiny babe too young to have a mind to remember with. Certainly the child never kissed her father, possibly she never touched him, for nurses carried her about on their backs when she was young and always had her well in charge, so that the samurai never had occasion to be mindful of her. The little she saw of him was "through the top of her head," for his appearance was the signal for profound obeisance. When he came to the room where her mother or the nurses kept her she bent herself against the floor like a letter Z that someone had pressed down almost flat, and dropped her face into the backs of her wee dimpled hands, so that should her august sire's honourable glance deign to fall in her direction all it saw was a bundle of delicate silks, a bare spot where the barber had shaved the crown of her head, and the fine black fringe of the tonsure round it. He loved her, Japanese-father-fashion, but it would have been undignified to display emotion toward her, or even to go to her funeral had she died.

Perhaps there was a yearning in Aya's heart that only loving arms could satisfy, but if there was she did not understand it. She could not miss what she had never enjoyed. If conventions shut in her life as a cage shuts in a canary's, she did not know that the condition was not normal. Her life would be like her mother's life. Why not? She had not thought about it, had not expected anything different. The "three obediences" would be all there could be in it; first to her parents, then to her husband and to his parents; and should she become a widow, she would obey her eldest son, or if she were without a son, whoever might be the head of her husband's family. "Why not?" again, for ever since there have been Japanese women it has been their business to obey.

Oka San had lived up to this teaching faithfully, and now that Dana San (Master), her husband, was dead, and his relatives were far away, Oji San, though inkiyo, ruled the household. His body, that of a warrior once, had long ceased to be erect, but his mind was bright as ever, and as he read aloud the passages from the "Whole Duty" his face behind his huge tortoiseshell-rimmed glasses was as wise as an owl's. The contrast between his words, squeezed out with an intonation quite in harmony with the text, and the appearance of his listeners, was both ludicrous and sad.

As to the mother-in-law, indeed she was an element to consider in the matrimonial equation in the days when Kaibara wrote—a quantity partly known and partly unknown, but with undoubted abilities for making trouble. Had there been newspapers then the paragrapher would have found her fully as useful as she is to-day, but it would have

been Mrs. Youngwife instead of Mrs. Younghusband
—a heroine rather than a hero in the tragedy.

If Oji San's words are true, the women before him, one so young and one past middle life, must be mistresses of the art of dissembling. To look less vicious would be impossible. One refuses to believe that they could "glare wildly round" even should they try. Oji San is surely wasting words upon them. But he means well, and they are so submissive.

"It shall be your duty when you go to your husband's house, Aya San," said the old man, "to reverence your father-in-law, and to obey him and your mother-in-law in all things as you have obeyed your own parents. Filial piety is the chief duty of a girl. You must give yourself up to their direction. It is well you have learned to boil rice properly, and to speak to your superiors always with your face to the floor, and to control that harshness natural to a woman's voice which, alas, is the cause of so much domestic infelicity. Your mother-in-law would send you back to us instantly if you served saggy rice or rice hard from insufficient boiling. That is a most just cause for divorce. Be ever mindful lest you bring infinite disgrace upon yourself and upon this house by inattentiveness to rice. Disobedience also will cause you to come back to us covered with ignominy; and in speech be careful every instant of your existence, for here is the truth as I will read it to you—the sixth reason for just divorce. 'A woman shall be divorced,' says the sage Kaibaru, 'who by talking over much and prattling disrespectfully disturbs the harmony of kinsmen, and brings trouble on her household.' Remember, too, that a woman once married and then divorced has wandered from the 'way,' and is covered with the greatest shame, even if she should enter into a second union with a man of wealth and position."

Surely Japan is severe with the girl who is not "up" on rice. Imagine English custom demanding that the young wife who does not bake properly should go back to her parents' house with a character as black as the bottoms of her first loaves, and a heart as heavy as their insides!

"But how about the husband?" someone may ask. "Where does he come in? What is there that he must do or must not do?" That is hard to say. The answer seemingly is, "Nothing." At least there is no "Otoko Daigaku," or "Whole Duty of Man." It is a pity. Japanese women should have an opportunity to write one, but to let them would be indelicate, and if they had opportunity they would not think of doing anything so impolite. If men wrote one—but they have no chivalry.

Aya San bowed low as Oji San closed his book at the end of each reading, and ejaculated: "Honourable Grandfather, your august words are honourable truth." Then she would pour hot water into the tiny teapot from the kettle on the coals, and give Honourable Grandfather a tall blue cupful of a mild beverage very different from the dark concoction one drinks in London.

After Honourable Grandfather, Bo Chan, the baby

brother, next needed her attention, and then there were her studies, for Aya San was ambitious. The spirit of New Japan was in the air, she breathed it in, and wished to learn something in the new schools the Government was establishing. This was hard to manage, for schools take time and money; not more than a shilling a month, perhaps, but one shilling out of every eight when there are four mouths to feed! No, it would not do. So she worked at her books at home. They were old books which she had borrowed from those of her girl friends who could go to school. Dog-eared and tattered they were, when Aya's friends had done with them and gone on to more advanced ones, but they were treasures to the little housekeeper; she studied them at nights, sometimes when she had only fireflies in a cage to see by.

One day a missionary from Tokio out "prospecting" stopped at the low thatched cottage of three rooms in which Aya lived, to ask some question as to the road he was upon, and heard Oji San's sepulchral wheeze as he read—

"Let her never dream of jealousy. If her husband be dissolute she must expostulate with him, but never either nurse or vent her anger. If her jealousy be extreme it will render her countenance frightful, and her accents repulsive, and can only result in alienating her husband completely from her and making her intolerable in his eyes. Should her husband act ill and unreasonable, she must compose her countenance and soften her voice to remonstrate with him, and if he be angry and listen not to the remonstrance, she must wait over a season and then expostulate with him again when his heart is softened. Never set thyself up against thy husband with harsh features and a boisterous voice!"

"That is rather more of meekness, I fear, than we Christians are wont to expect," said the missionary to himself; "but after ten years here I have come to believe that our Japanese sisters, heathen though they may be, have achieved it. I have learned something from them." Oji San continued—

"A woman should be circumspect and sparing in her use of words, and never, even for a passing moment, should she slander others or be guilty of untruthfulness. Should she ever hear calumny she should keep it to herself and repeat it to none, for it is the relating of calumny that disturbs the harmony of kinsmen and ruins the peace of families."

"Next to gospel that is the truth itself," agreed the missionary; "but why should it be 'for women only'?" and raising his voice he cried—

"Gomen na sai!" In a moment the "shoji" (the sliding paper door), opened, and Aya's pretty face appeared. The missionary made excuses for disturbing the august household, and then asked about the road. She replied sweetly and begged him to take a cup of tea, "most good for honourable weariness." Over the tea he asked more questions, and talked so long that he had to hasten back to Tokio when he left, lest he should miss his evening service.

A few days later he was out again, with an offer in writing from his mission to take Aya San into the mission school and give her an education free

JAPANESE GIRLS AT HOME

of all cost for board and tuition. Household duties, however, said "no" to this, though to the young girl the offer was as an invitation to enter the gates of the Blessed Country.

The man of God was sorry, but a month afterwards he established a station near Aya's home and saw her frequently. He lent her books, and under his direction her progress was extraordinary. The dog-eared volumes she had begun with were years behind her now. Twelve months later, after a public examination, she received a teacher's certificate from the Government, and that household's puny income doubled. She had fallen in love, too, and so had the missionary, but the romance ended soon. Both were eager to marry, but the samurai, Aya's father, had promised her to a friend's son. She had been engaged since she was two years old to a person she had never seen. The one who made the engagement had long since passed beyond, yet the engagement held.

But for the dead man's hand Aya might be among the new women of her land to-day. She did not stand still, however, for she is now somewhere between the old and the new; she has not shaved her eyebrows nor stained her teeth, though her husband is her law and her life. If there are other men in the world she does not know it.

Of the girls who lent her those old books, some are teachers in Normal schools and colleges, some have charge of kindergartens, some are governesses, some are nurses in hospitals, and a few are wives of officials, and give balls and receptions after the

European fashion, and wear European clothes, arrange their hair without the use of the perfumed cocoanut-oil paste of former days. They have long lists of male acquaintances, not one of whom is their husband, play the violin and piano, ride bicycles, play tennis, win prizes in archery, talk over telephones, and actually precede the men when entering a room.

CHAPTER XII

HAPPY NEW YEAR

JAPAN is the jolliest country in the world at the New Year. Gardner and I found it three times jolly, in fact. Each January 1, 43,000,000 subjects in the Land of the Rising Sun begin to paint not a mere "town," as a band of cowboys might, but the whole of the Mikado's Empire. The colour is naturally the glorious roseate hue of the Imperial emblem—The Rising Sun. This deep red harmony, they say, is eminently fitting at the beginning of the year; and that the painting may be well done, they administer three distinct and separate coats right lavishly.

The bottom or foundation coat is two full weeks in putting on. Joy flows in streams along the thoroughfares, swelled by rivulets from every house. All the city folk call on each other; all the country folk come in to help them do it; and everybody gives everybody presents. This may be called the official New Year. It dates only from 1870, when the Japanese Government changed its calendar to conform to that of the rest of the world. On the first of February there is a second coating—this is the New Year of Old Japan, still dear to the rural heart. All the country folk call on one another then, and many of the city folk go out to help them. There is less formality about this celebration, less éclat, but good-fellowship abounds, and joy is rampant for a week.

The third coating is given in good old Chinese style. Its date depends on the moon, as does our Easter festival. Each household celebrates by itself in part, and in part with outside friends; but this feast is more domestic, though not less sacredly observed than the two preceding.

The New Year season is the time to see Japan socially at its best. It is true there are no "kiku," as they call crysanthemums, nor plum nor cherry blossoms. The kiku comes in the autumn and the "sakura" (or cherry), and the "ume" (the plum) in April, both seasons when all outdoors is a garden-party, and exquisitely picturesque, but, with all its loveliness, it is only the outside one sees then.

To look into the homes and the hearts of all Japan one must be there New Year's Day. Business generally is suspended, both private and public. Doors open wide then, and hospitality, such as is unknown in Europe or America, is the rule without exception.

The jin-riki-sha coolie is the only one that works, but his task hardly is irksome. Waiting while his fare makes a call, he feasts in the kitchen with the cook, so that when night comes, though his load is rather heavy probably, he does not complain.

The geisha has her busiest season at New Year,

HAPPY NEW YEAR

but her work is always play, and she enjoys it quite as much as those whom she entertains. Her plaintive love-songs are never sung more sweetly than at the beginning of the year, when the heart of the nation warms anew. The geisha is very near that heart, and chirrups sympathetically.

At the first of the year the Emperor and the Empress receive for three days. On the first day only those of royal blood, the highest officers of State, and foreign diplomats, make their bows. Then follow in turn personages of lower degree, down to those who, having some title to recognition, are honoured with a gracious notification of the reception at the palace, but are expected not to come.

The Princes Royal and their consorts, after paying their respects to the Throne and to each other, in due order, according to degree of kinship to the Mikado, receive in their turn in petty state. The Ministers of State, diplomats, Members of Parliament, distinguished folk, and any foreigners who may wish to do so, pay their respects. These receptions are extremely formal, and everyone connected with them is glad they continue only three days.

The grand folk on the fourth day join the crowd, and, like them, go hither and thither to every accessible acquaintance, as ordinary people have been doing from the early morning of "Ganjitsu" (New Year's Day). Of course, no one can call on every individual of his acquaintance in the Empire, so he resorts to postal cards, which he despatches to all those friends whom he is unable to see personally.

He begins each card as follows, despite the fact

that in many cases he knows nothing of the honourable health, or of the weather, or of other conditions at the homes of those whom he is addressing:

"With the rigorous inclemency of the weather so increasing, I have the honour to rejoice at your august robustness. What I have to say is, august consideration honourably vouchsafed during past year, most humbly, most gratefully acknowledged, deign to continue the same and to pardon the contemptible selfishness of selfish me, for the unspeakable effrontery of venturing to address honourable you.   YOUR LITTLE IMBECILE ——."

This writing entails no little labour, for there is no type-writer for the Chinese characters which the Japanese use in correspondence. The pen or rather the brush strokes are by hand, sometimes forty of them in a single name. No wonder that in January some wrists are tired.

The calls, too, have their little peculiarities, for it is the callee, not the caller, who is the principal recipient of favours. With each call the caller presents a gift, usually some sort of food; but anything will do, even money. Boxes of eggs are in demand; so is "kasutera," or sponge-cake. Kasutera is from the Dutch word "Casteel" (Castile), for Spanish bread. The Dutch at Nagasaki in 1600 first taught the Japanese the art of making that dainty. Wine, beer, all sorts of canned goods, and articles of apparel are distributed too. It is a great season for the brewer, the baker, the confectioner, the distiller, and the hens.

As presents come in such profusion, they would

accumulate beyond control were it not for the custom of "passing along." It is not at all necessary that madam should eat all the eggs that are given her. That would be difficult, and to keep them long about the house would not be pleasant; so, after reserving whatever she chooses, she puts her card in each of the remaining boxes, and when her lord comes in for the fresh supply of gifts which he needs in order to continue his round of calls, she hands them to him.

Thus replenished, he starts out again, and madam at home gathers in a further collection. This keeps up for a fortnight, during which the kasutera and the eggs do not grow fresher. The dealers who supply these commodities, however, provide against damage to their reputations by pasting in the box of cake or eggs something to this effect: "This cake was baked at 11 p.m., December 31. These eggs were laid at 2 a.m., January 1, 'kotoshi' (this year)."

As these presents are passing along they often complete the circuit and arrive at the place whence they were first sent out, but it is only to begin the tour again. There is no rest for a Japanese New Year's gift until it is eaten or drunk or lost.

All one's tradespeople will call, too, bearing samples of their wares, commensurate with the amount of patronage each dealer has received. They present these samples with many bows and a request for a continuance of their patron's august condescension during the ensuing year.

While the shops are closed to business they are

open for pleasure, and there is a banquet in each home from early morning until early morning every day of the two weeks. And the tradesman hopes that all those who have honoured the shop with their patronage will call and bring their friends.

Foreigners seem to be particularly welcome at this time, especially Englishmen and Americans, for the common people like English-speaking folk. A man from England or the States might begin to feast early New Year's Day, and continue feasting until January 15, if he could endure it, even among strangers. The shopkeepers would show him more genuine hospitality than his own cousins would at home.

As there is plum-pudding at Christmas in England, and turkey for Thanksgiving in America, so there is "mochi" and "shirozaki" for the New Year in Japan. Mochi is good, and so is shirozaki. Mochi is made of rice boiled in fresh water and pounded in a mortar until it is dough, then it is rolled out like a yard of baker's bread, cut in slices and laid to dry till a slight crust forms, when it is ready to toast. Often, boiled beans are worked into the dough, till the casual globe-trotter might mistake it for a nut sweet.

Shirozaki is white and thick, quite different from the thin pale sherry colour of ordinary saké. It is sweet and wholesome, made of rice, with the body of the fermented grain left in.

The country-folk repeat these grand two weeks of celebration a month later, for they are slow to adopt new customs though they enjoy the official New

Year in town hugely, if they have opportunity to go. City folk, especially those who long for the good old days, are sure to be with their cousins in the country for the second feasting, and to stay a week at least with them. Then, when the moon changes, comes the oldest feast of all, and the country quiets down until another year is born.

This Far East custom of New Year calls, once so prevalent in England and in America, was brought to Europe by the Dutch merchantmen, it is said, who traded with Japan in the sixteenth century and after. But the Western world has been growing busier year by year, and finds hardly time nowadays for so much merry-making.

CHAPTER XIII

"CHITS" AND PERDITION

CERTAIN moneys Gardner had expected to collect when we ran down to Yokohama were not immediately in evidence, and we therefore had recourse to "chits."

"Deuced convenient things, you know," a globe-trotter remarked to us of chits; and he was right. Too convenient, if anything. Take, for instance, the man with a thirst and no money. He will find the Japanese seaport a joyous place. The combination so trying abroad is of no inconvenience whatever in those hospitable abodes; and, besides, those petty annoyances incident to having money always in one's pockets are done away with.

There you are always "good for a drink," or anything else. If you do not look too much like a sailor—a "Damyoureyes San," as the natives say—and are able to write your name, you need not worry. The secret of all this is chits. "Chits," being interpreted, means "joy made easy,"—joy and other things. They are one of the pleasantest curses known to man. Great and wicked was the brain that invented them. The owner of that brain is already responsible for hundreds of merry-making wrecks, who with all too much facility have drunk themselves to death on his ingenious plan. He has been their evil genius, but what he did was consummated with a liberality of manner that robbed death of half its sting.

Public opinion in the seaports is not pronounced enough to emphasise the line between the use and the abuse of chits. Among old residents there is opinion against the abuse, of course, but there are so many "transients" with homes that are far, far away. Among these, in a large measure, restraint is ineffectual, and so it happens that men, particularly young men, do feel freer than is safe. They are a genial lot, fond of outdoor life, well travelled generally, and well read, with charming manners, and hospitable, with a frank generosity that wins at once. They have leisure beyond the dreams of toilers in the West. They work harder now, perhaps, than formerly, those of them with occupation, but their custom was to come down to work at ten a.m. and to quit usually by four. Out of these six hours one and a half were spent at the clubs or in the great hotels, where chit signing is indulged in as a liberal art. In the races twice a year they rode their own horses, and out of respect to the turf, when the races were on, all business, even banking, was at a standstill. Wine flowed as fast as the laws of gravity allowed, but there was little cash in sight. The boys who served the drinks did not handle money. They pushed the bottle and a scratch-pad towards you, and someone signed. The chit then went to some hotel.

When a few months later you wished to pay, you would have some trouble in finding the slip to which you had put your name. Going from one place to another, at each the manager would say—

"I don't know. They may be here. If I find them I'll send them up to you. Let's see; what is your address?"

If you were sure he had them, you might pay and he would credit you. Then you owned the place. Whatever you bought thereafter he might not charge against you, but would say, "That goes to square us for what you paid against the chits I never found."

It is only globe-trotters that carry much cash in their pockets in Yokohama, and they soon give up carrying it, just as they give up eating rice-curry with a fork. Railway people and beggars are the only people who don't take chits, but the railroad, though convenient, is not necessary, and if one believes in the doctrine *similia similibus curantur*, he can pass beggars by also, and never know the touch of filthy lucre.

If you offer money to the barber, he may say, "Oh, wait till the end of the month. We can't bother making up cash now. Sign a chit."

At the tailor's you are asked, "Shall I send the goods to the club or to your hotel?" If you ask about payment, the reply is, "Oh, we'll send you a memorandum now and then, to let you know how you stand with us. But that is not a bill, you know.

"CHITS" AND PERDITION

Just let that run to your convenience, please. Send a chit when you like."

The jin-riki-sha man takes a chit from the hotel to which he has delivered you, or the hotel pays and you sign a chit. Every public-house in town passes out the little pad with the pencil hanging from one corner. Lodgings, meals, everything an hotel has to rent or sell to its guests, may be signed for on the chit. Nor is there anything that Satan can furnish to promote delirium or to coax the coming of old age that a little chit will not settle for.

He who has looked on the wine when it is red, and has studied the mockery of strong drink, need not moan in his first waking thoughts with despair, brought on by the recollection that his last penny went the night before, unless, alas, he is too shaky to hold the little pencil. But even then a promise to sign later will bring him what he needs!

There are settling days, of course, when the residents arm themselves with courage and go forth to pay their chits. Some men do this every two years. Others, who consider themselves patterns of regularity, square up bravely each first of January. Then there are men who have the names of the places where their chits are held arranged in groups, and each group assigned to a particular month of the year. At the first of each month they settle a part of their debts. This system sometimes gives chit-holders opportunity for guessing, though; for readjustments in the scheme of grouping one's chits will occur with even the best-intentioned signers, so that a holder who thought his money would come in January may find himself mysteriously moved into the December class, but that does not matter much.

Besides these annuals, bi-annuals, and monthlies, there is a class made up, it is said, of those who do not pay until they die. These men have life insurance policies, or assurance policies, to speak with local accuracy, and, being thus assured, they do not bother who holds their chits, or whether the chits were signed ten days or ten years ago. There are few men, however, who have signed chits steadily for ten years. Three years is generally the limit. A man can sign a barrelful in that time—a barrelful that stands for many other barrels empty. When the assured man dies, his chits appear, and straightway are paid, the first money collected from the policy going for this.

The number of chits not paid is large considered by itself, though relatively small. It is this fact that is the penniless man's advantage. He lives on the fringe or ragged edge of the crazy quilt of chits until he "loses his face," or drinks himself into the hereafter. When his "face" is gone he may sign no longer. He drifts into the Consul's hands, and is sent home steerage at his Government's expense. He may so dread the thought of home that he flies to the natives, among the disreputable of whom he must have some acquaintance, and in return for a modicum of seaweeds, fish, and rice-beer, teaches Peter Parley's *History of the World*, or possibly the art of mixing cocktails.

When he dies, the chances are that the foreign

residents will subscribe to bury him decently, and others of his class will mourn for him, hoping that some day someone will do the same for them. The class is one, however, that is less in evidence each year.

As the transient population of Yokohama increases, chit signing may disappear, although the habit is second nature to those who live there now. Here and there a man rebels, and swears that he will never sign another chit, but a temptation that is ever present is hard to resist for long. With nothing between a thirsty man and the drink he longs for but the scrawling of his name on a slip of paper, the chances are that the thirst will win. Other things, too, he may crave as keenly, things that will do him less good than a drink; the fatal paper makes it all too easy, and reform difficult.

"So they sent him out here to sober up, did they?" said a London newspaper man who was at tiffin at a club in one of the treaty ports one day, and was speaking to a friend of a youth whose parents thought Japan would do wonders for their bright but wayward child.

"Might have as well sent him to Hades to cool off."

CHAPTER XIV

THE CENSOR AND THE CRAFTY EDITOR

OKASHI SAN had given us a letter to a Tokio friend, the editor of a newspaper. He had been to Oxford, and to Harvard University in America, and we were eager to meet him, but inquiries at the address Okashi had given us were singularly unavailing. After much searching we found our gentleman in jail.

When I learned of the vicissitudes of his profession, however, I wondered how he had kept out so long. It was an occupation beset with difficulties indeed. Vexatious enough in all countries, in the Land of the Rising Sun it has been so uncertain that it is a marvel it was even possible. To an Englishman, and yet more to an American or an Australian, such uncertainty would be intolerable. The Japanese editor, like Brer Rabbit in *Uncle Remus*, never has known " what minnit's going to be the next."

In looking into the business I found that since the promulgation of the Constitution in 1889, papers had been suspended at the rate of one a week, while some of the more outspoken writers had grown so familiar with the way to the " honourable jail" that it was said they could go there blindfolded.

As was natural, after the war with China, the Japanese did some little talking about their equality to Westerners; but on the other hand, in the matter of the freedom of the press, they cannot fail to see that they are a century behind the times. This has been demonstrated in the trial of the editors of several papers, among them the *Tokio Shimbun*, for criticising the Minister of the Imperial Household. The trial aroused public opinion, and Parliament has passed laws modifying the rigour of press censorship to some extent. Still, to-day, an editor might as well commit hara-kiri, so far as his paper is concerned, as to give a line of army or of navy news, or say what he thinks the Government should do to hold back Russian aggression. Even in papers in the English language, which are published in the seaports, and are owned and edited almost exclusively by Englishmen, writers must go slowly. Before the recent treaties came into effect they did not fear the red pencil of the censor. Then they alone dared to discuss questions of State. Now, however, they must be as careful as the editors of papers published in the vernacular.

The list of "dont's," that is the list of things a writer on a paper must not say, is long, and, worse than this, no one outside the Bureau of Press Censorship knows what it contains. It is only by guessing and by bitter experience that an editor can approximate as to what to avoid. If a paper publishes an article that is not approved, the paper is suspended, and that is all there is about it. No reason is given. The disapproved article is not even mentioned in the order of suspension. Small wonder, then, that there is discontent, and that the cry for reform grows louder every day. And this cry is not without effect, for now Government promises to give editors a public trial when there has been transgression.

Here is a translation by Basil Hall Chamberlain of what the editor of the *Nichi-Nichi-Shimbun* says of the tribulations of journalism in Dai Nippon: "Newspapers and magazines are confronted by a special danger—the danger, namely, of suspension when their words are held to be prejudicial to the public order; and a suspension, too, against which there is no appeal. Article xix. of the Newspaper Regulations now in force says: 'When a newspaper has printed matter which is considered prejudicial to public order or subversive of public morality, the Minister of State for the Interior is empowered to suspend its publication either totally or temporarily.' Nor is there a word said in the regulations whereby the prejudicial or non-prejudicial character of a statement or argument is to be determined. It is sufficient that the official in question should decide, in accordance with his own individual opinion, that the statement or argument is thus prejudicial to public order, for a newspaper to incur at any moment the penalty of suspension, whether total or temporary. It is indisputable that the authorities are empowered by the law of the land to act thus. The Constitution itself gives them this power. The result is that we writers are constantly obliged, in taking our pen in

THE CENSOR AND THE CRAFTY EDITOR

hand, to keep to ourselves seven or eight of every ten opinions we would fain express."

When a paper ventures too far, and the censor is called upon to write the order of suspension, he is brief but polite—wonderfully polite. He puts the honorifics " O " or " Go " before each of the nouns and verbs. Prefixed to a noun " O " means honourable, to a verb it means honourably; similarly " Go " means august, augustly. So the order when it arrives will read somewhat as follows :—

"Deign honourably to cease honourably publishing august paper. Honourable editor, honourable publisher, honourable chief printer, deign honourably to enter august jail."

The honourable editor with his honourable coworkers bow low before the messenger of the censor, acknowledging the honour of the august notification, and then accompany him to the honourable jail, chatting the meanwhile of the weather, or of the flower shows, or of the effects of the floods on the rice crop. Centuries of breeding under Japanese etiquette have rendered it impossible for them to show annoyance. They do not know how.

When a paper has been suspended, the first intimation the public has of the fact is the quiet in the composing-room. Few places in the world where regular business is carried on are noisier than a Japanese composing-room. The amount of noise therein is determined only by the cubic capacity of the apartment. If it is a larger room, there is more noise; if a smaller, there is less; but in working hours it is always chock-full. The confusion at the Tower of Babel is there vividly suggested every day.

For the ordinary Tokio paper there will be at least twenty men and boys marching to and fro, each yelling at the top of his voice. There seems neither head nor tail to this confusion, but nevertheless each of these screeching persons has an object at which he looks intently while he parades about. This object is a line or stick of Japanese characters, for which he must find the appropriate types. It is something of a job to find all these, for to print even a four-page paper in Japan upwards of five thousand different characters are used. These require many fonts, which are crowded into a small space, that there may be as little travelling as possible.

The "devil" goes about these fonts with a waltzing motion, there are so many corners to turn, and always with his eyes fixed on his stick, as though it were a sacred relic. Indeed, to the stranger in the street below who looks up through the long windows which reach from floor to ceiling, it might seem that a religious dance was going on, and that the devotees were wrought well up to the frenzy point.

On going inside one finds an old man sitting in a corner reading copy, and cutting it into strips with what looks at first glance like a pair of sugar-tongs, but which are really shears. As each slip falls, a "devil" grabs it and starts off on his pilgrimage singing at the top of his voice the names of the characters he seeks. He has to pronounce the name of each character aloud in order to know what it is, for he understands by hearing rather than by seeing, and his own paper would be unintelligible to him unless he read it aloud. As all the other imps yell also, he has to be vociferous in order to hear himself.

When he has collected the types for all the characters on his slip he gives them to the head-compositor, a learned man with goggles, who puts in the particles and the connecting words, and hands the completed forme to a pair of proof-readers, one of whom sings them to the other. As soon as the proof is ready, the paper is made up, all hind-side before, it would seem to a foreigner. The reading lines are perpendicular, and the columns run across the page from right to left, the first column beginning at the upper right-hand corner of what in a European paper would be the last page.

There are no headlines nor any display advertisements. The paper consists generally of a leading article, a lot of news items—more or less untrustworthy, a jumble of advertisements sometimes printed on the margin of the sheet, and a section of a continued story. There is almost no telegraphic news, and little correspondence either local or foreign. Occasionally a student who is studying abroad will send a letter, but not one of the six hundred and forty papers and periodicals now published in the Empire maintains a regular correspondent anywhere, not even in the large Japanese cities.

The news department is as largely "fake" as it is in any of the issues of the "new journalism," but it is the leaders, after all, that make one wonder why the paper is published.

With the sharp red pencil of the censor pointing

at him, ready to be thrust into him behind his back at any moment, the editor has evolved into a man skilled in the art of saying nothing, or, at least, what reads like nothing to the uninitiated. He is a marvel at *double entendre*. But with all his cleverness he is caught so often that he has become inventive, and has devised artifices whereby he has hoped to escape.

The most successful of these was the dummy or "prison editor," as he was known in the Oriental sanctum. This functionary had an easy time. He had nothing to do on the paper, never wrote a line, but when those who did write said anything that the censor judged might mean something, and the paper was suspended, the prison editor stepped forward, bowed low, and said, "What augustly must be, probably augustly must be." Then he trotted off to prison. This scheme worked well for a long time, but after a while the censor demanded that the principal three men connected with the paper should go to the "honourable jail." Three dummies were more than any paper could afford to maintain, and so there are no proxies now.

But the remarkable thing about these papers is not that they are so meagre in every department, but that they exist. The first Japanese newspaper was published in 1872, by John Black, an Englishman, who founded the *Nisshin Shinji Shi*. Before that there had been only occasional terror sheets which the "yomi uri" (the native chapmen) hawked about after a particularly bloody murder, or a catastrophe, such as a great fire, a flood, or an earthquake.

Black's paper was followed by others, among them

THE CENSOR AND THE CRAFTY EDITOR 117

the *Kwampo* or official Gazette; the *Tokio Shimpo* and the *Kokai*, semi-official; the *Mai Nichi Shimbun*, the *Yomi Uri Shimbun*, and the *Ubin Hochi Shimbun*, all Liberal; the *Jin Shimbun* and the *Ninkin Shimbun*, Radical; the *Nihon* and the *Chusei Nippo*, Conservative and anti-foreign; the *Fuzaku Gwaho*, an interesting illustrated record of manners and customs; and the *Maru Maru*, a comic paper inspired originally by *Punch*. There are also prominent the *Chuguai Shiogio Shimpo*, a commercial daily; the *Jiji Sin Shimpo*, Imperial; the *Tokio Nichi-Nichi-Shimbun*; and in Osaka the *Asahi* (*Morning Sun*) and the *Mainichi*, which are read widely in the south of Japan.

The Japanese reporter makes about as much money as the Japanese policeman—that is, about twelve shillings a month. In Tokio some of them make more, and in the smaller towns they make as little as eight shillings a month, but twelve shillings is a fair average. They are not sent out on regular assignments as a rule, but are given a roving commission. The editor tells them to get news, real news if there is any, but to get news; and they never return empty-handed. A good news-gatherer is rare among them, but the "fakir" is plentiful enough and really clever. Interviewing can hardly be said to be popular. The people do not understand it and do not like it. Japan is esoteric, and doesn't tell what it knows if it can help itself. Still, there are interviews in Japanese papers. Politicians have themselves interviewed occasionally, and "globe-trotters" usually submit.

All the papers use the written language, which

differs from the spoken language both in its grammar and in its vocabulary. Mr. Chamberlain says that the Japanese are still in the condition of Europeans of the twelfth century: "They do not write as they speak. A man may know the spoken language thoroughly, and yet not be able to understand the daily paper when it is read aloud, nor even the note he has just asked his native clerk in his office to write and to send up to the house, announcing that he will take up a friend to 'tiffin.'"

Speeches are taken down in shorthand, but are almost always translated into the written language before they are printed. The one exception to the rule is in the Record of Parliament speeches, wherein the words are published just as they were uttered. When this Record first appeared the rural members were filled with consternation, for there they saw held up to the public eye all their peculiarities of provincial dialect. Old men as some of them were, they got themselves teachers and set about learning to speak like townsfolk.

This Record is the beginning of a tremendous reform which students hope will lead to the disuse of the written language, first in newspapers, and finally in books as well. For the spoken language is the living language, the language of the people. With the present Parliament a new order of things will be established in Japan, and the freedom of the press must follow in due course. Ministers of State incline to think that the time is almost come. But it is well to remember that while the present laws are cruelly severe, as judged by Western nations, they

THE CENSOR AND THE CRAFTY EDITOR

are, as Professor Chamberlain points out, not so severe historically speaking, because it is hardly a quarter of a century since freedom of speech was denied to the Mikado's subjects, not theoretically perhaps, but to all intents and purposes. It was a capital offence to memorialise the Government. Those who did so—and history gives many instances—were wont to write what they had to say in the form of a letter to the Prime Minister, and then, calmly kneeling at the gate of some public building, commit "hara-kiri," or, to use the polite term, "seppuku." The police, who may have stood respectfully at a distance while the act was committing, would find the letter on searching the body of the suicide, and report its contents to the Minister.

CHAPTER XV

BOBBY

ON our visits to the honourable editor in the august jail we saw much of Junsa, the police officer. We liked him. So do all foreigners.

This is natural, for the Japanese Bobby is a gentleman by birth, a model of courteous dignity and a good fighter. In consideration of these qualifications the Government gives him six yen a month, or about twelve shillings. He is a gentleman, because he comes from the highest of the social grades—the samurai—and until 1871 was a military retainer of a daimiyo, as the feudal lords were called who ruled over the provinces of Japan. He was born to the use of the sword, and even now, except in seaports, it is his weapon as well as his badge of office, though rarely is he compelled to use it.

Samurai, according to the dictionaries, means "military class," "warriors," or "gentry." Recently the Chinese word "shizoku," of precisely the same meaning, has come into vogue, why, no one knows, for it adds nothing to the significance of the idea. The samurai lived in the daimiyo's castle, and received annually an allowance of so many koku of rice,

A SAMURAI WITH PRISONER

according to his importance and the richness of the province. Japanese still reckon incomes in koku. The samurai's business was to be a gentleman. In Old Japan all gentlemen must be soldiers and all soldiers gentlemen. To-day it would not be quite wrong to say policemen. The samurai attended his daimiyo on all occasions, and fought for him whenever there was trouble with another daimiyo. He was the embodiment of loyalty, and would give his life deliberately to avenge an insult to his lord.

Mitford's *Story of the Forty-Seven Ronins* shows how he could do this. The ronins were samurai without a master. In Mitford's story, which relates a fact of Japanese history, they carried out a scheme of vengeance requiring months of preparation, knowing all the while that, whether they failed or succeeded, the Shogun would sentence them to hara-kiri.

So to-day, the samurai, with all the instincts of ancient chivalry and this twelve shillings a month salary, promenades the highways and byways of Nai Nippon armed with a sabre and a ball of twine, and preserves order the like of which no other country in the world maintains. The sabre is in lieu of a policeman's "billy," and the twine he uses instead of handcuffs.

It is interesting to watch Bobby as he deftly weaves a net about his captive until he looks as though he were wrapped up in a hammock. This weaving has an esoteric significance, doubtless, as no need of doing it is manifest. Etiquette in Japan is against a captive's trying to escape after he has been informed courteously that he *is* under arrest and should augustly condescend to accompany his captor to the police-station.

The policeman always says, "Go men nasai" ("August pardon deign"), and the culprit, as he stands patiently to be woven in, replies, "Do itashimashite" ("Oh, don't mention it"). When the weaving is over Bobby has the culprit "on a string" and, holding one end thereof, escorts him to the station, where the captor salutes his chief in military style, and the captive bows low and declares he is mortified to be the cause of so much trouble. Both ends of the string are heard from, and the chief then decides whether to fine or to dismiss, or to hold the offender for further examination.

Bobby wears a military uniform—white in summer and blue in winter. He always salutes when a foreigner speaks to him, and will walk a half-mile with one to show the way. He will not accept a tip. His instincts and the rules of the Police Department forbid his doing so, and then, besides, there is the Government pay—twelve shillings a month, on which he feeds and clothes his family.

He will take charge of a foreigner in search of an hotel, and will escort him to the best lodgings to be had, where he will caution mine host against overcharging the guest. In the monthly bazaars that are held in the streets leading to various temples in Tokio, Bobby is ever watchful lest the dealers ask the foreigner too much for their wares. So vigilant is he that the stranger often makes a better bargain than a native could.

One of them through clever detective work secured

over one thousand yen that a native had stolen from a foreigner, and refused the gift of money that gratitude prompted. After much persuasion, however, he accepted a kimono, though not before the American had received special permission from the Police Department to make the present.

In Yokohama and the other seaports, where the policeman does not carry a sabre, he handles his "billy" quite as well as any foreign policeman. He is wonderfully dexterous in the use of this as the sabre. Professor Norman, late of the Imperial Naval College of Japan, with whom fencing is a hobby, has studied fencing of all sorts in England, France, Germany, Austria, Turkey, Persia, Siam, China, and Japan. He says that the Japanese policeman is the most dexterous swordsman living.

Even with his club he will enter a drinking place where a half-dozen men-o'-war's men are having a rough-and-tumble fight, and arrest them all with celerity and ease. Jack has a wholesome dread of the little man in blue, and trembles when he sees the "billy." It is an odd sight to see him staggering to the station-house in charge of a man whom it would seem he could pack under his arm. It is like an ant taking home a beetle.

The entire police force in Japan is under a single head, with the chief offices in Tokio and a sub-department in each province. The chief is a man of extraordinary powers. His officers command such respect as only military men enjoy in Europe, and the entire system is as efficient, probably, as can be found in the world to-day.

CHAPTER XVI

PLAYHOUSES, PLAYERS, AND PLAYS

THE Secretary to the Chief of Police, a young Viscount who spoke English well, and who had conducted us on our first visit to the august jail, took us to the theatre one morning, and we spent the day there. We went often after that, and on the west coast brought criticism on our youthful heads by the keenness we displayed in studying the stage. The influence of Count Inouye's garden party, at which the Mikado was present and saw Danjuro and other great actors, had not reached Etchiu. But we persisted in our researches and found out several things. One of the first of our impressions was that a man needs gymnastic eyes and a laminated throat to be an actor in Japan. The eyes count for more, however. A good eye-wriggler need not want for a position, nor need the owner of an indiarubber face, for "making faces" is an art with the Japanese stagefolk.

The achievements of these artists are illustrated accurately by the contorted countenances shown on the cheap paper fans so plentiful in summer time the world over. These fan illustrations, be they ever so grotesque or weird or fantastic, are exact representations of stage scenes. They are not exaggerations. The garments shown in the pictures conceal effectively all outline of the human form, but they are stage costumes such as Japanese actors wear to-day; and the faces, in spite of the distortion they display, are portraits of theatrical stars which anyone familiar with the native theatre would recognise immediately.

I believe there are no better equipped actors in the world to-day than those found on the Japanese boards. The theatres, too, such as Meijiza and Kabukiza, in Tokio, are excellent, with their electric lights, their revolving stages, and their simple yet beautiful scenery. Many of the plays would be intelligible to an audience that did not know a word of Japanese. Danjuro, whose real name is Horikoshi Shu, and Kiugoro the great comedian, speak a world language and will make you laugh or cry at will. It is a pity they cannot be prevailed upon to make a foreign tour. They would draw well.

Their versatility is marvellous. They play comedy, tragedy, and farce, in either male or female parts, with equal facility and happiness. They were born to the stage, as were their parents and grandparents before them for ten generations, and have taken parts from the time they were of sufficient size to be seen by the spectators. With such inheritance and such training it would be strange if they did not excel.

In spite of all this excellence, however, it is only recently the theatre has been in good repute in the Mikado's Empire. Count Inouye, then Minister of

Foreign Affairs, gave his famous garden-party in the autumn of 1887, for the purpose of elevating the stage. His Imperial Majesty Mutsu Hito attending, set the seal of supreme approval upon a profession which before that time had been taboo with gentlefolk.

The records of the census-taker show the position of actors under the old régime. This official counted them, "ip piki, ni hikki, sam biki," etc., when reckoning the number of men in a theatre. That seems harmless enough until it is explained that, in counting in Japanese, "ichi, ni, san, shi, go, roku," etc. (one, two, three, four, five, six), certain auxiliaries to the numerals are used, according to the kind of things that are being counted. For instance, human beings are "mei" or "nin," and are usually counted "ichi nin, ni nin, san nin," etc. Flat things, such as sheets of paper, are "mai"—"ichi mai, ni mai," etc.; houses are "ken"—"ik ken, ni ken, san ken," etc.; boats are "so"—"is so, ni so, san zo," etc.; and living creatures, except human beings and birds, are "hiki"—"ip piki, ni hiki, sam biki, shi hiki," etc. Actors, therefore, came under the general classification of beasts.

Until recently the upper classes kept away from the theatres or went there only in disguise. But, in spite of this, good plays were produced and, financially, at least, the profession prospered. To-day distinguished actors are received in the homes of persons of noble rank.

The Japanese theatre is the only place left in which one can study the ways of Old Japan. Though it retains many of the ancient and grotesque traditions

PLAYHOUSES, PLAYERS, AND PLAYS 127

of its early days, it is accurate in presenting customs that else long since would have passed from memory. Its language, too, is formal and archaic, and the intonation of the actors almost terrible. You will not find such language or such voices anywhere off the stage. A half minute's attempt to imitate the sounds the native actors produce would give a Westerner bronchitis. The throat is contracted, the veins swell, and the blood seems ready to burst from every pore in the tragedian's face. Then the eyes roll, individually and independently, one up, the other down, one to the east and the other to the west, or only one gyrates and the other rolls, until only the white shows. The iris disappears entirely. This is done especially when the eye-wriggler wishes to demonstrate that he is bold and bad. When you see him you will believe he is.

The bearing of the actors, cast for kings and queens, is comical. It brings to mind descriptions of the old miracle plays. To walk like ordinary mortals would not do for royalty or for personages of any sort. They must strut like a German recruit breaking in. It is something to remember the entrance of a Chinese Emperor as he comes down the aisle through the audience. At each step his foot rises quite to the level of his chin, while his revolving eyes appear to be two inches in diameter.

All this seems childish enough to ruin the effect of the most excellent acting, but it does not. In battle scenes, particularly, the exaggeration is extreme. Japanese actors die hard—on the stage. It is appalling to see how long they last. They stagger about, still slashing at each other, after they are shot as full of arrows as a porcupine is full of quills. The first arrow would have done for them anywhere but in the theatre. Stage blood is over everything; but the audience delights in gory scenes, and the actors must be "an unconscionable time a-dying." Arms and legs are lopped off. The wounded roll about making terrible grimaces, and dummy limbs, appearing through the floor, twitch and jerk about the stage in a way not pleasant to weak nerves.

In place of the calcium with the coloured slides, a black-hooded mute with a bamboo pole, at the end of which is a lighted candle, moves about with much agility and illumines the chief actor's countenance by means of the sputtering dip. To the stranger this jet-black elf is rather an attraction in himself and a serious distraction from the play, but after a while the spectator grows accustomed to the imp and is oblivious to his presence, and the actor holds the entire attention.

Another distraction is the orchestra, and a dismal one it is to the uninitiated. Its performances should have a chapter to themselves. It is usually at one end of the stage, behind a screen, which conceals the appalling physiognomies of the members, but does not add harmony to the sounds. The "music" and "singing" continue without a pause all the time the curtain is up. The songs are indescribable, for the tones are something between the squealing of a pig and the wail of a lost soul. It has a certain fitness, however, one discovers after several hearings, especially in the ghost and goblin acts—and during the carnage of the battle scenes it is quite in harmony with the interminable slaughter.

The general appearance of the Japanese stage is much the same as the stage in a foreign theatre. The stage itself revolves, but otherwise the scenery is managed much as it is in this country. The actors, when they die, are attended to by the hooded elves, who see them safely away behind blankets.

The audience does not applaud by hand-clapping; it shouts the actor's name. It is a comfortable audience, with any amount of time. Plays begin at eight o'clock in the morning and continue until seven in the evening. Different theatres give performances at different hours, however. In some places the doors open only in the evening. The floor of an empty theatre looks like a checker-board. When the theatre is empty it looks much like a theatre in this country. The difference is, that there are no stalls. The entire seating space is partitioned off into squares by means of railing, about a foot above the soft-matted floor. This gives the orchestra and pit the appearance of a checker-board. Each square holds a half-dozen spectators. In the balcony often there are boxes. Generally the spectators have tea-caddies and their lunch with them, especially in the country. Folk often take gourds of saké too, but in towns the tea-houses of the neighbourhood provide all sorts of refreshments at moderate cost.

Between the acts the spectators visit about the house and exchange saké cups. Occasionally some of the actors come down to see them. They always receive a present, just as geisha do. All sorts of hawkers of food and drink run about on the railings while the curtain is down, offering their wares to the spectators.

Smoking goes on all through the performance. There is no formality of dress, nor is it unusual to see a spectator curl up for a nap to carry him through a portion of the play he does not care for. When an act is ending, the curtain-man announces it by a nerve-shattering racket, made with two hard pieces of wood which he beats together. As the curtain falls, all the children in the place rush for the stage and have a merry game of tag. Often they crawl behind to see what is going on. No one interferes with them nor shows the least annoyance at their pranks. The stage is theirs until the clatter-man sends the curtain up again.

Queer as Japanese theatrical methods are they are far ahead of the methods that obtain in China. The Chinese theatre is familiar to some extent abroad, for one may see it wherever there is a Chinese colony, notably in San Francisco, in New York City, and in various places in the colonies; but the Japanese play has stayed at home, though Kawakami and Yakko came over here after various adventures in the States, and made a hit in London, and especially at the Paris Exposition, where they showed that a good Japanese troupe, aided by a clear translation with intelligible notes, could do exceedingly well. Their manager knew his business.

At present there is little differentiation in the foreign mind between things Japanese and Chinese. This annoys the subjects of the Mikado, for they are not related to the people they recently conquered. Neither in blood nor in language is there any connection whatever. In Japan, foreigners enjoy the theatre; but in China, hardly. There is no way of stopping a Chinese play. Once it is fairly started it runs until the theatre is burned down, or the actors die of old age. Many Japanese plays, however, are of the same structure and duration as English plays. Where the theatre is open all day the play is broken in two, and between the sections a sketch, something like a curtain-raiser, fills in.

On the Japanese stage dead men are taken off by the attendants. They do not jump up and trot off in the merry Chinese fashion. The orchestra in Japan is not all tomtom, either; nor is it on the stage, mixed up with the actors. Indeed, some of the performances on the samisen are exceedingly clever and full of life. Japanese scenery is well-nigh perfect, and the revolving stage, of which the Chinese know nothing, saves much time.

Recently, too, in Japan, mixed troupes are allowed. Men and women may appear on the stage together. This is not so in China, nor can it be said to be in great favour as yet in Japan, because the old ideas are not gone yet. Japanese plays are extremely realistic, more so than would be allowable were both sexes on the stage together. The appearance of women in companies with men certainly would curtail this realism, and it is thought by some that drama would lose thereby.

Since the war the theatre has prospered mightily,

and prices have gone up. Still, eight shillings is not a great sum to pay for twelve hours' use of a good box, and a chance to see much that is ludicrous but also much that is admirable and instructive.

One evening Gardner beckoned two of the performers to our square. We had a cup of saké with them and asked them to come to see us the next day, Nichiyobi. They did so. In fact the whole troupe came, so that we had to adjourn to a teahouse not far away where there was more room. The news that we were entertaining players spread, and I fear we lost caste sadly, but we had a grand time nevertheless. Several of the townsfolk whom we knew came also, and though they may have held an actor in contempt no one would have suspected it from their actions. They exchanged saké-cups with the men from the theatre, played chess with them, and later, when the geisha had arrived, joined in a sort of grand march, which the professional folk led. There was never such a Nichiyobi before in Etchiu, I will warrant. We felt we were working along the lines of the distinguished chief of the Foreign Office.

The dismay that came upon us when first we saw how many the two whom we had invited were, changed rapidly to joy under the stimuli of the occasion—stimuli, by the way, which the master of the tea-house kept constantly in evidence. We were pleased with our good work.

"I wish it continuing always," said Okashi. Then he had a cask of saké set out in the road where several individuals had collected, and the theatre folk helped to apportion it, and in this kindly work our other guests assisted, until someone ran away with the cask. We retired, of course, without saying good-night, feeling sure that Okashi would not let the evening drag. Gardner's last remark was, "Don't you think the stage will be all right if only the people on it are elevated?"

CHAPTER XVII

"MUSIC"

BESIDES the actors and the plays that we studied in the theatres, "gaku" attracted our attention. It was so persistently bad we could not help becoming interested. We had some of the "gakunin" at the house one afternoon for a close inspection.

Okashi San treated them with some consideration, for, as he said, their fame was great, but Gardner and I had trouble in keeping up to Okashi's dignity of bearing. I do not believe either of us ever had such another hour in our lives. We were full of internal cramps through trying not to laugh, and the pain was such that it was equally difficult to restrain our tears. To sit there in apparent peace, while trying desperately not to do two things so opposite in kind, was a strain our nervous systems did not soon recover from.

"Gaku" is a Japanese word which the dictionaries translate "music." If you ever hear any gaku you will wonder what is the matter with the dictionaries, and will suspect their trustworthiness ever after, consulting them with hesitancy.

GAKUNIN

"MUSIC"

Gaku should be translated, "a series of irregular and disconnected vocal squeaks accompanied by strings twanging out of tune and interspersed with caterwauls." That would be comprehensive and exact, except when the vocal squeaks are omitted. Without the squeaks gaku is the same in kind— unqualified and wilful discord, but not so much of it.

The dictionaries would have you believe also that the vocal squeaks are singing. They say that "uta" means song, that "utau" means to sing, and that "O uta utau nasai" means "Honourable song to sing condescend," *i.e.* "Please sing a song." That is pretty poor guessing, even for an English-Japanese dictionary. "O uta utau nasai" should be translated "Bring me two earfuls of cotton." With your ears well stuffed you may listen to gaku without going mad. Otherwise much self-control is necessary.

There are many kinds of gaku in Japan, each of which is worse than any of the others, with one exception that may be made occasionally in favour of classical gaku. This kind is esoteric, so very esoteric at some of the Shinto festivals that only the motions of producing the discord are made, and the soul-piercing uta is left out as well. These are the only times you will not desire cotton.

When court musicians, the most classical of all gaku folk in Japan, break out into sound, the atmosphere is torn to ribbons. There is something in the result to suggest that striking picture, "The March of the Conquerors." One sees the chief killers that the world has known advancing between the parallel lines of dead, and also a tidal-wave full of cats, pawing helplessly in the foam and clamouring for succour. Yet all this pleases the Japanese ear, so that the more discordant of the gakunin acquire fame and are talked about. But the gaku itself never attracts notice. No one discusses it, no one cares who composed it.

Classical gaku is a thousand years old, likely two thousand, for it came over from China back somewhere in the sixth century, and has not grown better ever since. No one knows how long it afflicted China before leaving for the Land of the Rising Sun.

After watching our guests we understood how, now and again, a gakunin dies of heart failure or of congestion of the brain. The men strained so in squeezing out the uta that their necks swelled and the veins stood out as large as clothes-lines. Their eyes were bloodshot, and their faces a dull brown purple. Each growled and gagged and yapped until he reached the convulsion point. One of the gakunin unlimbered his neck and thrust it out like a chicken reaching for a worm, and the blood receded and left his face the colour of washed-out leather. Then the other did the same; and then they alternated. I felt it would be foresight to order coffins for Gardner and me at once, but I could not speak.

When several gakunin unite in crime they pay no attention to key or to harmony, for such things do not concern gaku. They do, however, keep common time together — the only time the Japanese know anything about. Each "singer" strains and exhausts himself independently of the others, in whatever way he can produce most discord. Gardner estimated that with each word the gakunin squeezed out he expended enough energy to wind an eight-day clock.

As there is no notation for any but the classical gaku, all gaku must be handed down by word of mouth and learned from the living teacher. Wee girls sit for hours each day before the instructor— usually a woman past the flower of her youth, no longer in demand in the tea-houses — and practise at the "break," the point just between the lower and higher register, where all the possible raspiness of her little voice can be brought to complete development.

All Japanese uta are rendered at the "break." This is a cruel surprise to the foreigner when he first hears it, for nothing further from his expectations well could be when the dainty maid sits down before him, with a winsome smile, her samisen resting on her knee, and her taper fingers playing up and down the strings. He is utterly unprepared for the series of weird, discordant notes, which sound more like an incantation to "blue devils" than what the interpreter assures you it is—a love-song.

After this attempt to give the reader a suspicion of what gaku is like, it need not be a surprise to hear that both Professor Chamberlain and Koidzumi Yakumo (Lafcadio Hearn) say that a Japanese Bayreuth is unthinkable. Still there is some hope. The speaking voice of the natives is soft and sweet. The vocal organs are all there, and the ear does not appear to be abnormal, for with the violin and the piano Japanese students studying abroad have done good work. An effort is making now to build up a school of foreign music in Tokio.

Those who would like to study the "music" of Japan, and have not at hand the appalling facilities Gardner and I enjoyed, cannot do better than get Mr. Piggatt's beautifully illustrated volume, *The Music and Musical Instruments of Japan*. Mr. Piggatt finds in the native instrumental music "some reflex of the national grace, some prettily quaint flashes of melody and curious phrase repetitions."

According to Confucius, China had something like real music once, and Japan probably learned something of this in early days. Too bad she did not develop it. The idea of the man who said "Let me write the songs of a country and I care not who makes the laws" is an old one. The great Chinese philosopher saw the truth in it twenty-four centuries ago. He said, "Harmony has the power to draw heaven downwards towards the earth. It inspires men to love the good and to do their duty. If one should desire to know whether a kingdom is well governed, if its morals are good or bad, the quality of its music shall furnish forth the answers."

What must a Boxer band be like?

CHAPTER XVIII

BLOSSOMS ALWAYS IN BLOOM

SEVERAL times there were geisha in our theatre parties, and of course they were present at all our feasts. No Japanese would think of giving a dinner without these innocent hetæra, whether it were to be in a public tea-house or in a private dwelling. That is, of course, unless his feast were in the foreign style. Then the native buds and blossoms would be quite out of place. They are indispensable for the native celebrations though. In five years I never saw a gathering for pleasure without them. They make everything go successfully, so cleverly, and with so little friction.

The mission of the geisha is to make life merry. Her whole education is to that end. She can dance and sing, and play on all sorts of instruments; she knows the best stories and the latest jokes; she is quick at repartee; the games she doesn't know are those that have not yet been invented. She is as graceful and frolicsome as a kitten, her manners are exquisite, and she is as beautiful as—well, as beautiful as a geisha. Only dead folk can withstand her charms, and it is doubtful about them. Her mirth is the best of tonics. It will mend one when anything ails the health. She cures everything, that is to say, but diseases of the heart. These the geisha has been known to aggravate. In truth she doesn't need more than half a chance to put a heart in a terrible way.

In Japan everyone is always entertaining someone! Few things happen that do not demand a feast. Consequently the geisha is never out of sight for long. She appears at the festal place soon after the earliest arrivals, or about two hours before dinner is announced. It is the custom in Japan, for guests come ahead of time instead of on the minute or a little late.

The first sight you have of her is as she bows low at the threshold, her hands palm down on the floor before her, and her face pressed close against them. She says, "Omina sama gomen kudasai," which means, "Honourable Mr. and Mrs. Everybody, august pardon deign." "Irashai," call out some of the guests as they look up from the chess boards or tiny packs of hana cards with which they have been playing. Irashai means "welcome," and the geisha enter to take possession of the teapots and to "jolly" everyone as they serve the gentle stimulant.

Their entrance is not the least bit wobbly, as one might think from the performances wherein foreign actresses try to represent the geisha. A singer's robes (kimono) are quite too long for any gait like that. The European stage-folk must have got their ideas of the Japanese foot motions from a study of native women dressed in European style, certainly not by watching Yakko the Entrancing. Japanese

IN JAPAN EVERYONE IS ALWAYS ENTERTAINING SOMEONE

women do walk queerly when their feet are encased in high-heeled boots. Their gracefulness is gone then, the glide that holds their sandals on becomes a shuffle, and the inward swinging of the right foot, caused by the side pull of the kimono, which clings so closely to the figure, developes into pigeon-toe.

When a geisha has served tea all round, and had a dainty bit of chaff with everyone, she glides off to the kitchen to see that the saké, sashimi, the kwashi, and other things are ready. She has an artist's eye, and can serve raw fish — which sounds anything but appetising to Westerners—so daintily on a lacquered tray that you simply have to try a little.

As soon as the portions are arranged, she glides back to the guest-room with china bottles full of hot rice-beer. She puts bowls of water full of tiny cups at intervals about the room before the guests, who have ranged themselves along the border of the apartment. To each one she offers a cup, and then pours out the saké with a bow, saying, "Please condescend to drink one full." With the wine come kwashi, that is different kind of cakes, which she serves on little oblong brazen dishes. It seems like beginning with the dessert, but it is quite the proper way in Japan.

While the guests are busy with this appetiser of kwashi and saké, the geisha goes to the corner of the room and puts on her evening robes. She does not go out of the room to do this, for she is a lightning-change artist, and as the daytime garments are sliding from one shoulder the clinging folds of the evening gown are upon the other, and with a bit of a shrug and a wriggle the thrush becomes a nightingale.

An assistant binds the robe with a broad sash, tied in a square knot behind (which, by the way, is the original bustle), and she comes purring among the guests once more, bearing trays loaded with lacquered bowls and china cups, containing soups and fish of many kinds, until before each guest there is a fair foundation for an art museum. Then she brings out her "samisen," a three-stringed, square-headed "banjo," and, plucking with her "bachi" or "plectrum," tunes it to the weirdest key that sounds were ever known to give. The sad melody of waters beating on a foreign shore as the surf-sprite sings of loneliness—such is the geisha's music and her song. As she plays, her younger sister dances. Not as we dance here, nor as any of the imitation geisha dance. There is little motion, but much harmony of line, as she turns about and postures and wields her fan so deftly that it seems to hover in the air as if it were a moth circling above a candle-light. Her posing tells more clearly than any words might do the story of her elder sister's song. It is a love-story always. It could not be anything else when a geisha sings it. It is not "Chon Kino," however, unless she is a seaport geisha, and a cheap geisha at that; for "Chon Kino" is sung in the lowest places only, and except in seaports there are no low places in the whole Empire.

"Chon Kino" is for sailors, and men-of-war's men, whom the natives call "Damyoureyes San." It is sung by a class of girls unknown in Japan before foreigners arrived. Its origin is not Japanese at all.

It came from the early Dutch, who taught it to their temporary wives at Deshima, Nagasaki. It is really part of a game of forfeits, after the manner of "Simon says 'thumbs up.'" The usual forfeit after "Yokohama, Nagasaki, Hakodate, hai," is to take off one piece of cloth. This forfeiting continues until there is not anything more to take off. Whoever has the most on at the end of the game wins.

Hilary Bell is quite right in his opinion of the teahouses of the seaports and of the geisha who pose therein. He says that those geisha would make a good man blush. But do not think that the genuine geisha—those of inland Japan—are not as honest and pure-hearted as any woman in the world. It is a mistake to suppose that "geisha" is synonymous for easy virtue.

Geisha dancing is often pantomime, and where a half-dozen of them dance together they form a theatrical troupe in themselves. They would be delighted with their counterparts in foreign theatres, but they would be amused, too, at the funny differences. Fluffy hair is not Japanese; petticoats are not worn under kimono; high heels would play sad havoc with the delicate tatami that cover Japanese floors; waraji, or rough straw sandals, are not worn in the house except in the kitchen. (Geisha either go barefoot or in tabi.) Kimono fold round the body with the left side over and the right side under, unless the wearer is a corpse. Real geisha never hug each other nor even hold hands—much less kiss. Geisha do not cross their hands over the breast when they bow, they bend over as though giving a back for a game of leapfrog. The hands are pressed against the knees and the spine is horizontal.

And another thing is conspicuous by its absence in the European imitations. It would be a sad thing for the dear little girls if they had not even one smoke in a whole evening! Geisha carry pipes of gold and silver bronze, with which they enjoy ippuku, one whiff, from time to time taking a pinch of mild tobacco from the leather pouch each one has slipped into her obe.

Moreover, it would surprise geisha to know that they could be bought and sold easily, as the foreign play-writers represent. A geisha is usually indentured to a teacher when she is young, or perhaps the teacher pays the parents for a release, and then adopts the child. But even then she is not owned. Her contract, if she is indentured, stipulates a sum on payment of which she can be released. If she is adopted, and later runs away and marries, there is no legal cause for her recovery. Indeed, she does this very thing occasionally. Many a Japanese official of high rank has been proud of such a helpmeet.

A GEISHA

CHAPTER XIX

SIGNS OF THE TIMES

ONE of our amusements as we strolled about the towns we visited was to study the signs along the streets. There was human interest in them. But a few of those we saw were unique. Yet in spite of their oddity they are truly signs of the times; there is some history in telling how they came to be, for they are of the period when Japan was stepping from her old clothes into her new. Feudalism with its daimiyos and military retainers was disappearing, and so were caste distinctions. The Government had just established a system of schools on a German-American plan, with much English and much military drill, and had set all the youth of the nation to school together to gain Western knowledge. Children of the four classes of society—warriors, farmers, artisans, and merchants, and even of the outcast "Etta," met on a common footing for the first time.

Hasami San, the son of Kami San the barber, was the equal of the son of the samurai, and the barber was happy in the fact. Kami San knew nothing whatever of foreign ways. He was of the old régime, but he had perfect faith in his Government, and if Government favoured foreign ways surely they were good. And this English language, too, which all the schools were teaching, so that no matter where one went he would hear of the great Peter Parley and his History, of Lord Macaulay, and Clive, and Warren Hastings, of George Washington and the cherry tree. Was not Hasami studying about these things every day in classes side by side with gentlefolk? Surely he must put up an English sign to show the world that his abode was the home of learning as well as other houses, even those of great pretensions. His son should have the job—Hasami San who played with the children of fighting-men and of the owners of many rice-fields, who knew the characters for writing "Eigo"—as he called the foreign tongue, and who even at this moment was in military uniform, drilling to become a soldier in the army of the great Mikado. The barber's nose was high.

Kami San talked of these things to his friend Hige San while Hige was receiving a ha'penny's worth of treatment. He had gone entirely over Hige San's face with his thin narrow blade, even to the eyelids, and now had hold of his friend's nose and was reaming the hair from his nostrils with a tiny gouge-shaped razor, that few but a native barber would dare to use.

"The times are changing," he said, as he rolled Hige's head a little to the right, twirling his gouge, "and when Hasami has leisure from his studies in the coming rest days of the school, he shall show by the new knowledge that I have the pride to make changes too, keeping by the times closely in my business."

Here he lifted Hige San a little, saying, "Augustly condescend honourable head to elevate," and began to shave the ears. He did so deftly and thoroughly, both inside and out. When this was over, and he had taken a run round the neck, he struck a tuning-fork and put the handle, which had a knob on its end, first into one ear and then into the other. The tuning-fork gives the customer the impression that he can hear himself purr, and so makes him happy.

Hige San arose shining and beaming, paid his two sen, said that Kami San was augustly gloriously expertissimo, and declared that an English sign over the sliding doors that made the front wall of the shop would be an honour to the neighbourhood, a sign, in truth, befitting the new era which Tenshi Sama, the Son of Heaven, had deigned to honour with the name of Meiji—the Epoch of Enlightenment.

"Oh, it will be of course a most unworthy and disgraceful object, as is everything in my miserable shop. But the new language from the wonderful people of the West, that it is which I wish to place on high," replied the polite Kami San.

The "rest days" Kami had referred to came soon, and Hasami San had the leisure of his first vacation. He had learned the alphabet, "aye, bee, shee, dee, ee, efoo, jee," etc., and could tell a "dee" from an "oh" almost every time. Besides, he knew many words and short sentences from his first reader. He could not pronounce "el," it is true, the nearest he could come to it was "eroo," as is the case with the general run of Japanese to-day; such words as "literally" and "literary" are beyond them, but he could draw characters skilfully, English letters being simple compared with the Chinese intricacies that youngsters learn to write so deftly with a brush.

So when his father explained the sign idea to him he set to work diligently, and by the time the holidays were over he had produced an ornament over his father's Chinese lettered sign that filled the old man's heart with joy. It was in three lines, which he printed and shaded beautifully. It read—

BARBER
TO SHAVE BEARD OR TO ORESS
HAIRS WAY.

Kami San was the proudest man in town when he gazed up at the completed work. He gave a dinner to celebrate the event, and had all his friends in for the day. Saké flowed. There was raw fish, boiled fish, grilled fish, and cuttle-fish in profusion, and even the hardy little fishes that submit to slicing up alive. In the evening he had lanterns all over the front of his shop, with special illumination for the sign. Geisha strummed their samisens and danced and sang, and the guests had so good a time that many of them forgot all about going home until Kami San awoke them in the morning.

The fame of the sign spread. Soon it was the envy of every one of Kami San's brothers in the "hairs way," and of the tradesfolk generally. Those of them who had sons that had learned the "aye, bee,

SIGNS OF THE TIMES (a)

shee," commanded them to do as Hasami had done, and those who had no sons sought to engage Hasami's services. Kami San would not hear of his boy's neglecting his studies of the wonderful Eigo, however, nor the military drills. He was busy, too, he said, for customers flocked to him, so that he had to hire two more assistants, and he needed Hasami himself whenever the youngster had any spare time.

As he said to Hige San one day, as he was shaving carefully over the tip of his friend's nose and giving a curve deftly to his eyebrows, he knew when the honourable good thing came his way, he was a respecter of signs and would not do anything to make a good one common. Except that his son had explained to him by means of a dictionary what his sign signified, he did not know its meaning, but its influence as it shone down on the passing throng was agreeable to his ideas, and he proposed not to meddle with it.

Kami San's lack of assistance did not hinder matters much, however. The sign craze was on, and it lasted longer than the rabbit craze. But then the Government put a stop to that, whereas it has never interfered with signs. English lettering appeared in Yokohama, Tokio, Nagasaki, Hakodate, Kobe, Kiyoto, and hundreds of other places, even at the tea-houses along the great highways where the jin-riki-sha men stopped for a sip of tea and a whiff from their tiny pipes.

"The tas are restful and for sharpen the minds," read one of these signs.

And another: "The Genuinely bier buy the health for drink."

And a third: "Of smokes our tobacco is preasure to our Tongue and give the Healthiness to Hers and Hes! Also All People by It."

These little notices in unexpected places relieved the monotony of a journey on a dull day. Their passing will leave a void. Some of them have disappeared already now that the railway has come, and the old Kaido with their inns do little of their former business. But those in the towns remain, except where they were, like the language of the "Damyoureyes San," far too frank. The camera has caught them, and should Kami San and Hasami San be taken up in a chariot of fire, their work would live. An "Etta" who was once an outcast, but is now "Heimin," that is a member of the great class that includes all but officials and nobles, expanded under the radiant announcement over the entrance of his leather shop—

To Trade Hair-Skin Sort Shop.

An entomologist of some repute in Yokohama, who supplied collectors of insects and also silk raisers with their "seeds," ornamented the front of his place of business with his name and the words—

Butterfly and Worm Merchants.

(Does the plural imply that this man has been leading a double life?)

The man who safeguards against sun and rain declared the fact publicly as follows:—

A Shop the Kind of Parasol or Umbrella
and Sticks,

and either of "parasol" or of "umbrella and sticks" he had great variety.

Japan looked askance at butchers in the early days of the new order. Beef and pork were taboo pretty well all over the country. Even now it is not easy to get animal food in the small villages of the interior, where some Buddhist priests still declare war against flesh and wine. But medical advice following a cholera scare has had much influence, so that one may see this sign to-day exposed boldly to view over a shop—

Cowmeat and Pigmeat.

In a country where there has been much raw fish, especially salmon, and not particularly good drainage until William Kinimond Burton took to teaching it sanitation, troublesome ailments would occur. To one of these Mr. Swiftriver had turned his attention with success. His sign read as one straight line—

Tape-Worm Swiftriver Shop.

Mr. Pinecape, who dealt in coals, took the public into his confidence and confessed the secret of his success. Beneath his name and address are these two lines—

Honest, Indistorious make the Cont
inual Prosperity.

Mr. Seedsmall, who dealt in so-called temperance drinks, which the Japanese call "gun water" because of the "pop," got hold of a dictionary in which some-one had translated the names of his beverages into Japanese phonetic equivalents. These Japanese syllables do not conform with extreme nicety to English sounds, principally because none of them ends in a consonant, but always in a vowel, and none of them has the sound of "l" in it. This is the English part of Seedsmall's sign—

RAMUNE SOUDA SASUPRE ZINZINBIYA JINJYAE-L,

which one sees at a glance to mean Lemon Soda, Sarsaparilla, Ginger Beer and Ginger Ale.

The brilliancy of official uniforms attracted the attention of a tailor, and he sought to make business amongst the men of the army and navy and the Government. His sign read—

GOLD TAIL SHOP.

Posterior decoration, apparently, was his speciality.

Another sign, that of a tobacco merchant on Ginza, the Bond Street of Tokio, was probably the best known in the capital for half a dozen years. It was not amusing, for it merely declared the maker's brand and where one could find it on sale, but it was ubiquitous. The merchant had taken the contract to water the city's streets from one end to the other on all dry days the year round. The brilliant red carts his coolies pulled about told everyone that

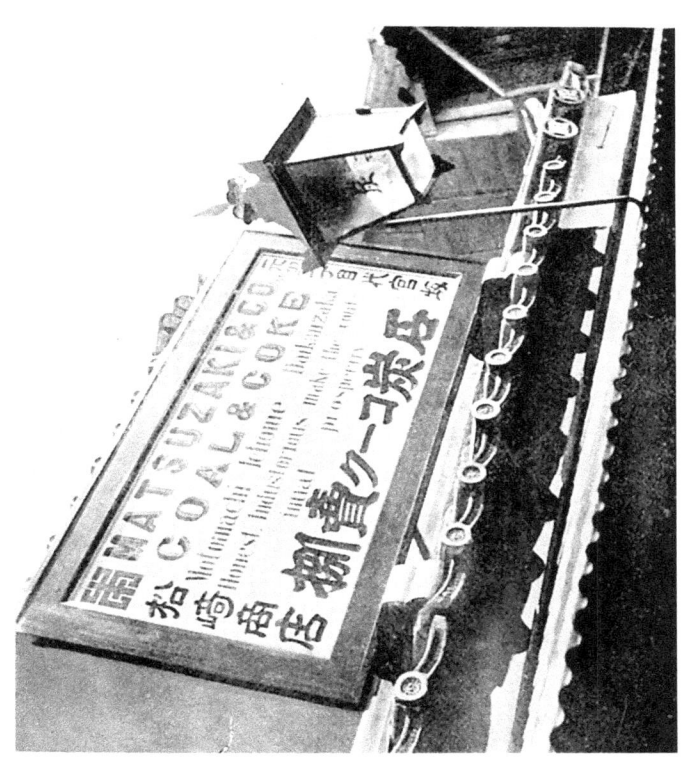

SIGNS OF THE TIMES (i)

in the tobacco business Mr. Pinemountain of the Ginza was supreme.

And so one might go on indefinitely quoting signs, labels on bottles and cigarette packages, the covers of books, and what not, all of them strange and some of them incomprehensible, yet all of them signs of the effort of Old Japan to become New Japan, an effort that has been triumphant.

CHAPTER XX

BOWS AND BALLOTS

GARDNER and I had the good fortune to be in Japan at the time of the first election the country ever had. It passed off with the greatest decorum and the absence of anything approaching ostentation, or even excitement, but it was not without some amusing aspects.

One wonders how the officials stand the strain. Election inspectors, for instance, must have rubber backs. They need them, for on voting days they have, at the lowest calculation, five hundred and twenty thousand bows to make, and now the franchise has been extended they will soon have to "ojigi" five times as often. That is a great deal of hinge work, and demands elasticity and lubrication, especially as ojigi does not mean a mere nod of the head. To be done properly, the body must double at the hips, folding after the manner of a two-foot rule. The "tachiainin," therefore, as the inspectors are called, no matter how automatic their early training may have made them, have no easy work on balloting days. When night comes, and the polls have closed, they climb into their jin-riki-shas and go home, to be shampooed by some blind "amma" and restored to life.

Five hundred and twenty thousand bows is a conservative estimate. It allows each voter only one ojigi, which is ridiculously low, for it is hardly conceivable that a voter should approach the inspectors who are seated behind the ballot boxes with less than half a dozen foldings, and etiquette naturally demands that the inspectors should fold, too. It is safe to allow three ojigi for each voter, and to declare boldly that every general election day in Japan has witnessed inspectorial doubling to the extent of one million five hundred thousand, or enough to supply the most energetic saint with genuflections for a lifetime. The new franchise, by similar reasoning, implies seven million five hundred thousand bows. Allowing a hundred foot-pounds to a bow, the energy folded off into space on voting days is found to be seventy-five million foot-pounds; or two thousand two hundred and seventy-two horse power.

It costs something to be polite, and it takes time; but time is plentiful in the Land of the Rising Sun. A Japanese needs about a quarter of a minute to ojigi. At this rate one man would be occupied continuously for 345 years 6 months and 14 days if he were to do all the folding himself.

Japan's population is something over 43,000,000. In area the Empire is about a quarter again as large as the British Isles, and speaking roughly it has one-third more of population. Only about twelve per cent. of this land is suitable for cultivation. The people, therefore, are crowded together, and large land holdings are not numerous. This accounts in some measure for the few voters in Japan at present, because the franchise was limited to men at least twenty-five years old, who paid direct taxes on land or on incomes of at least fifteen yen.

As an instance of a result of the operation of this law, Tokio, the capital, with a population of 2,000,000 has had only 7000 voters, or one to every 285 of the inhabitants. Almost all of the men entitled to vote have availed themselves of the privilege. The "kikensha," or "stay-at-homes," have been rare when compared to those in some of the elections here in England.

Voting is a semi-private, semi-public act, performed with much solemnity and no disorder. No one besides the voter and the inspectors is allowed in the polling booth while the function is in progress. The inspectors are the Mayor, or the headman of the district, and two or four other men chosen by him. They may be all of the same political faith, and, if inclined to do so, could manipulate the ballots to their own advantage materially. The law says nothing about bi-partisan Inspection Boards.

Another opportunity these officials have to help their friends along is in advising the voters how to vote. They may even fill out the ballot for him, if he does not wish to do it himself. His education may not extend to Chinese characters, and not caring to use the humble syllabic form, he begs the inspectors, with many ojigi, to do the names of the candidates for him in Chinese.

The ballot-box is almost an idol in the eyes of the

newly enfranchised natives. Indeed, they approach it with a reverence beyond that accorded to the temple images of Buddha. They are used to Buddha's images, but the ballot-box is still mysterious. In the eyes of the older natives it is a fearful matter for a private citizen to take it upon himself to make suggestions to the Government. Indeed, it is a manifestation of effrontery which in former days would have been punished by death, not only of the presumptuous citizen but often of his entire family. A ballot is certainly a suggestion, and so the old men stand in awe of it.

CHAPTER XXI

THE FLOWERS OF TOKIO

IT rained fire one night when we were in the capital. The air was full of flying shingles all ablaze. A beautiful sight to those with tile roofs over them, but hardly so if one were under thatch. "Tokio no hana," said Okashi, who had appeared the day before to ascertain our whereabouts. Translated literally, "Tokio no hana" means "Tokio's flower," translated freely, it means "fire." Fire is the flower of Tokio. Any Japanese carpenter will tell you that, and the bigger the hana is the better he likes it, for the more work there will be for him.

The carpenter ranks high in the artisan class, and in the popular mind Daiku San, as he is called, is still next to samurai, above the farmer and far above the merchant. He is therefore an important man, and when he is happy it is well to rejoice with him. Do not be vexed if you find him purring at your front gate as you rush out to notify the nearest policeman that your house is on fire. Rather tell him where the saké is, and beg him to help himself

THE FLOWERS OF TOKIO

and to take home what he does not drink as a present to his family.

He will do his prettiest in building a new house for you a few days later, and describe you to his co-labourers as a man of noble birth. Thus stimulated, the product of their labour will be excellent, and you will stand well with the community. In Tokio it is expected that a house will burn down about once in seven years (in some sections once in three years was the rule). There are plenty of exceptions, but rents are calculated on this basis. The owner reckons to get his money back with interest in that time, and then is quite ready to build anew.

A large fire in Tokio means good times, and a picnic always. The first thing a man does when he is burned out is to banquet all his friends. His credit is good under the circumstances, and a lack of ready cash is no hindrance to festivity. The more houses he has lost the greater banquet he will serve, and Daiku San will be much in evidence. He will assist in opening a koku of saké with generous dexterity, and will stand by till the last drop of the forty gallons has been distributed. He will aid in the distribution of balls of rice, neatly rolled up in jackets of raw fish, assuring each guest in turn that there is nothing like the fires that bloom in the spring, and that in Tokio it is always spring.

Figures do not lie, but in statements about fires in Japan they are misleading. A "griffin" reading in the *Mail* of a fire of one hundred houses, would think it a conflagration; but nothing less than one thousand is a conflagration in the Mikado's Empire, and a thousand make only a small one.

Bishop Williams of the American Episcopal Church looked out of his study window one pleasant evening watching a fire two miles away, and then retired to dream that the inevitable festivities of the morrow were interfering with his mission services. Three hours later his boy aroused him with the words, "Conflagration's wrath encroaches precipitately," and the good Bishop escaped in a robe not prescribed by canon. His dreams were all too true. Eighteen thousand houses disappeared in smoke, and Tokio was on a spree for two weeks. The greatest fire of all was away back in 1557, when over one hundred thousand people lost their lives.

Houses in Japan, however, signify less than in England. They are really roofs on pegs. The walls are sliding doors—"amado" on the outside, along the outer edge of the "engawa" or verandahs; "shoji" along the inner edge, which shut off the engawa from the living-rooms; and "karakami" or fusuma. All these can be lifted out of their grooves easily and carried off. Even the tatami are not fastened down, and they can be hurried away if there is a half-hour's warning.

All but the poorest houses have "kura," alleged fire-proof buildings, near at hand, into which everything of value may be stored away. These kura are of mud, plaster, and tile, and look to be impervious to heat; but the radiance of "Tokio no hana" is often too much for them, and they crumble into dust.

TOKIO

THE FLOWERS OF TOKIO

Fire engines are used to throw water on the firemen, not on the fire. That would be an utter waste. Few of the pumps, which generally are worked by man power, throw more of a stream than ordinary garden hose—just about enough to keep the firemen soppy and steaming. With his heavily padded "kimono," short in the skirt and bound to his waist, like a Norfolk jacket, his combination of tights and leggings, his blue mitts and pointed hood, and his long, barbed pole, Hitashi, the fireman, prances about in the smoke and the glare of the flames, pulling down everything to clear a path to leeward and so starve the fire. He looks like a devil, but he is only an acrobat.

Whenever there is a lull he will perform on a bamboo ladder—standing on his head on the top rung, and doing other difficult feats. He will be in for the picnic, too, along with the carpenter. On January 4 each year the firemen give a grand parade in Tokio, and do their clever tricks at frequent halting-places along the route.

The combination of kerosene lamp and earthquake produces many "Tokio no hana," and similar blossoms in other parts of Japan. Instinctively everyone runs to the lamps when the house begins to shake. Another cause of fire is the lucifer match, still in use among the poorer people.

A record of Tokio fires in the last two hundred and sixty years shows the district where they are most prevalent. This is called the fire district, and within its boundary shingle roofs are prohibited. Tin roofs are not yet introduced. There is, however, a greatly improved system of waterworks in Tokio, and with hydrants and better engines "Tokio no hana" may some day be a legend only.

At present, however, it flourishes, and is taken as a guarantee of joyous times—a truthful herald of prosperity.

CHAPTER XXII

IN THE KINDERGARTEN DAYS

OUR life on the west coast, especially when we were among the mountains with the Noto folk (most of whom had never seen a foreigner), helped us to understand what Japan had been, and to appreciate the gigantic work she has accomplished in recent years. The difference between the Japan of to-day and that of two-score years ago astounds one. She has done in forty years much that other nations have been four hundred in accomplishing. Her system for this accomplishment was marvellous. She had, for instance, the greatest kindergarten that ever was, greater than ever will be again probably. It was a kindergarten that included a whole nation both young folk and old, but chiefly it was for those who had attained their growth.

This kindergarten for grown-ups was unique. What other country in the world ever reorganised its "Society" over night, and ordered "everybody as was anybody" to begin living on an entirely new plan at once? That is practically what Japan did. She was just emerging from feudalism, the feudalism of the Far East, which represented a social order developed during centuries in which the outside world was shut away by laws of extraordinary stringency. Then foreign powers demanded treaty rights. Japan awoke. The civilisation of the West fascinated her as she opened her eyes after her long rest, and she determined to win for herself a place in the first rank of the nations of the world. She has been accomplishing her purpose, to the wonder and admiration of all.

To understand how much she has done, one must consider what she was some thirty-five years ago, and compare her condition then with her condition now. She was as feudal in 1870 as Europe was in 1500. She could not then find entrance to the comity of nations. Now she is a world power. Thirty years ago Japan knew practically nothing of Western customs, though she had a most elaborate ceremonial, one that provides for all possible emergencies of her own social conditions.

Many of these ceremonies were of great dignity, impressiveness, and even beauty, but they were quite out of harmony with European customs, and she decided to throw all overboard and to start again, to forget in a day all she knew of that formal picturesqueness which a thousand years had been developing. The samurai, or gentleman, laid aside his swords, those symbols of the spirit of Old Japan, which he held dearer than any price in gold could purchase; he gave up his silken robes; cut off his queue; let the hair grow on the crown of his head, and put himself into pantaloons and a frock-coat.

Here appeared some of the amusing features of the transformation. He bought a silk hat as an aid to the new civilisation, a tile that settled down and wobbled on his ears as though coaxing his head to grow. This hat he delighted to brush the wrong way. In those days anything did for a shirt, and the laundry-man had not arrived. When he did come he had to explain what his business was, and why folks should patronise him. Sometimes the man of New Japan went the frock-coat one better, and put on a dress-suit whenever he went forth. He was determined to prepare himself for the time when his country should rank as high as any European power,— should be the England of the East,—and if clothes would do it, it should not be his fault were that ambition not accomplished.

To the foreigner it looked a bit odd to see a man of forty and a youngster of four toddling down the Ginza of a summer morning in swallow-tails and chimney-pots, but their action was significant. It meant that Old Japan was dead. Sometimes these dress-suits had pink linings. One man, a copper miner, who had prospered in his business, gave to each of his coolies that had served faithfully in the mines one of these pink-lined suits as a New Year's gift. The coolies were delighted with the garments, and wore them proudly along with their "kasa" or umbrella-like headgear.

The disappearance of the old customs went on rapidly — and what a spectacle the disappearing process offered onlookers. In the transformation from old to new there was much that was sad, much that was joyous, and a little, necessarily, that on the surface was ridiculous.

Government had established its gigantic kindergarten (and in Japan, the land of topsy-turvy, a kindergarten for men and women is not a contradiction), it had brought foreign instructors from the world over, in each department, and had sent a steady stream of students abroad to study in America and Europe. As these students returned, the Government dropped off the foreigners, until few indeed are in Government employ to-day—though many are living comfortably at home on pensions after twenty years of service in the Land of the Rising Sun. Japan owes them much, but there is gratitude on both sides.

The "Kobusho," or Board of Public Works, which went out of existence in 1885, had charge of bringing in whatever Japan wished from the world outside. Marquis Ito, often Prime Minister, had charge of the Kobusho in early days, and Viscount Hayashi, now Minister Plenipotentiary at the Court of St. James, was Ito's right-hand man. The work gave them grand opportunity for learning foreign business-methods, but the clerks did not carry out our instructions as to orders going abroad quite as a clerk in an English office would. One order to the Kobusho's London agent read as follows:—

Urgent. Send to Tokio at once as follows:—
    1 Professor of Electrical Science.
    1   Do.   Mining.
    2 Blast Furnaces.

IN THE KINDERGARTEN DAYS

And in due course the London agent forwarded an invoice declaring that he had sent out for Yokohama, Japan, by steamer *Maru*, four items as per order, to wit—

    1 Professor of Electrical Science.
    1   Do.   Mining.
    2 Blast Furnaces.

Both of the learned companions of the blast furnaces are in England now. They did well by Japan, far better than the furnaces, which became part of a steel plant that cost the country 6,000,000 yen (£600,000) and came to nought.

The Kobusho was a busy place. Its duty was to furnish the stuff—mental, moral, and physical—for equipping some 35,000,000 to 40,000,000 people with a bran new civilisation. It went in strong for scientists. It imported all the kinds there were. Tokio was as a white ant-hill. Engineers swarmed over the city and the country round. Government contemplated a minute survey of the Empire, and bought a full equipment for a splendid surveyor-general's office in the capital, together with a great number of instruments for the surveying parties. The temporary office was of wood, and there a large corps of engineers worked for a year or so. Government had engaged them for six years, or until the job should be over. It found the work difficult and expensive. One night the office burned down and its contents went up in smoke. To get out new materials and then begin all over again "would be a great bother," said the

Kobusho, so Government thanked the engineers kindly for their work, paid them in full for six years, and they returned to their respective countries.

The Government scheme of Europeanisation included cooking in its kindergarten course. It encouraged beefsteak and rice curry and bottled beer. This gave rise to a unique lot of foreign signs and labels, such as "Bottled by Pale Ale & Co" on an imitation of a famous English stamp. Over one shop was this: "Rendezvous pour la Garde Imperiale, sale for a plat of food, sale for a glass of wine." Not far from this was this combination: "Literary Coffee House cafe de Billiard." (Billiards, called "Tamasuki," is a delight to the Japanese, who are expert players.) Another sign was: "A Sole Manufacturer of Confection"; and another, though not referring to food, was "Iron Foundry"—it was over the gateway of an Eye Infirmary. Basil Hall Chamberlain, in his delightful *Things Japanese*, has given many more.

Some of the signs that one used to see in Nagasaki, an English publisher would not venture to print for sale. Nagasaki is a seaport, the only kind of place in Japan that possesses "dives," and these dives stated their business frankly in language the dive keepers had learned from sailors. These keepers had visiting cards, equally frank, which they distributed smilingly.

With such misunderstandings of what the envied Europeans held to be proper, as well as what they held to be improper, were other misapprehensions. A not unnatural digression from *de rigeur* was to ladle out soup into finger-bowls. Finger-bowls are much the shape of the pretty lacquered cups in which

IN THE KINDERGARTEN DAYS 169

Japanese serve their soup. The soup at a European food-feast might come to the table in a tureen, or a wash-basin, or in anything that would hold soup. Indeed, there were strange vessels on the Tokio tables at times, and the confusion as to the purposes of European earthenware utensils gave foreign guests various sensations of mirth, astonishment, and even horror.

In the early days of the kindergarten, foreigners travelling in Japan went to the hospitals and to the chemists for their beefsteaks and their beer. This was because Japan was Buddhist, and the inhabitants generally would have nothing to do with either of these things until medical men introduced them. These physicians and surgeons, with their ideas acquired abroad, were shocking infidels in the eyes of the populace at first. But when the "infidels" pointed out that the large and fair and strong barbarians, who "knew everything," ate beef and drank beer—and did not have the cholera, the natives gave heed. Now one finds beef and beer the country over.

It was hard for the Japanese to drink milk, however, harder than it is for Americans to eat high game. But here, too, the medical man prevailed. Foreigners drank milk, therefore the natives would. Officials set the example nobly. Every morning at eleven o'clock the milkman called at the various Government bureaus and made his ostentatious rounds. Not an official escaped. Each one received his proper portion of the potent potion, and drank it—a liqueur-glassful. At the "Kaitakushi Jo Gakko," or Girls' School, belonging to the Colonisation Bureau in Sappuro, on the northern island of Yezo, the young women early learned to wonder at the ways of foreigners. The mistress of the dormitories made each drink a mixture of egg and claret, like the American claret-flip, every night before retiring. The girls did not like it, but "no flip no futon" was the order, and up so far north as Sappuro futon are desirable.

With the coming of the railways and the trams there were many things for the kindergartener to learn. One was time. They had had the most indefinite appreciation of that. It was odd to them that trains would not wait, that 12.0 would not do well enough for the 11.45, or that the engineer could be so absurd as to start up at 3.29 exactly. To the native mind, "exactly" did not mean "exactly exactly," it meant approximately, that is to within thirty minutes or an hour, or on the same morning or afternoon. The trams, too, were disobliging. They kept to a regular route, and would not diverge for those who wished to do a little shopping a quarter of a mile or so round this turning or round that. The guards had a hard time of it trying to explain clearly that a tram was different from a jin-riki-sha. Guards at the railway stations had their troubles also. The natives persisted in leaving their clogs outside just as they did when entering a house. It was a great bother for the guard to get all the shoes into the coaches before the train started. He could not pretend to sort them, and pairs that should have gone half-way only often went to the end of the line.

As soon as the dress-suit and the frock-coat had

IN THE KINDERGARTEN DAYS 171

established themselves in favour, along with the white gloves, which for some time all officials wore to their respective bureaus in the morning, they became imperative. A certain General who chanced to be in Tokio at the time of the Mikado's Chrysanthemum Show at Akusaka learned the value in which the Japanese held the frock-coat. The show is by far the most wonderful of its kind in the world, one of the single plants there has over six hundred blossoms growing on it. The General loved flowers, and admired the "kiku," as the Japanese call the chrysanthemums. He had an invitation to go to the show, but his frock-coat was in Yokohama and there was no time to get it. Without one, nobody not possessing wings could get in, and even then he would not be allowed to alight. So the General, rather a large man, borrowed a coat from one of the Japanese officials at the Foreign Office. Thus arrayed he was a picture to remember. The only wonder greater than that the General got into that coat is that he was able to get out. But he saw the flowers. After that, so long as he stayed in Japan, he would not go across the road unless he had a frock-coat ready for emergencies.

The Empress set the new fashion for women, and appeared at Chirini's Circus in magnificent "yofuku," or foreign dress, which she had ordered from Berlin. She had also a German Master of Ceremonies to educate the Court in the art of how to behave though uncomfortable. Corsets and all came with the new apparel, and it was rather difficult at first to persuade the wearers to use them right side up, the Japanese figure being somewhat of an inversion.

With foreign dress came the idea that a woman was an individual rather than merely a thing, and that she should receive consideration. In her native kimono she had always stepped aside that the men might go first. Men had gone first always in all things. But with the aid of the yofuku Japan was able to illustrate the idea that women should take precedence. Chivalry depended on the petticoat, and as chivalry was a fine thing in the West, the Japanese must have it. So in skirts the Japanese lady led the way, and received attentions that bewildered her, for never before had she spoken to a man other than her husband except at the distance of several mats, and with the greatest possible formality.

She had dancing lessons, too, for the Government saw that balls were an institution in all foreign capitals, and naturally it wished Japan's representatives to be prepared to enjoy them in the proper spirit. All the Cabinet Ministers, the Governor of Tokio, and the great swells generally, each gave a ball every winter, and the officials went as part of their duty, but it was hard work. The floors of the ballroom were so slippery. It was much more fun to take a run and to slide across them as boys go on the ice than to spin about top fashion, holding a woman round the waist for the first time and dancing with her publicly. It must have been strange for a gentleman of Japan who had never so much as touched a woman's hand before in his life, or had never paid even a formal call on women-folk. Except with geisha at some dinner or other, he had never had conversation with a woman other than members of his household, yet here he was with his arm round a woman he had seen for the first time that evening, who was fully as embarrassed as he, for she knew how to talk to other women only, and he must whirl round and round to music that was altogether unintelligible to him, and must try to be entertaining at the same time. Truly European civilisation was wonderful!

The members of the staff at the "Gwaimusho," the Foreign Office, had to pay particular attention to all things relating to European customs, for they were to make up the various diplomatic corps abroad. So they learned French, frock-coats, dress-suits, and dancing, as hard as they could. English they knew, of course, for all the schools taught that more than any other one subject. French they needed for the Court, and for diplomacy, and to read the names of the strange things they had to eat. They mastered these details with remarkable thoroughness, and to-day the Japanese diplomat is at his ease the world over—an interesting fact when one considers all his country has had to learn to teach him. He should be as proud as one can be, righteously. A glimpse at the past must make him so.

Less than two-score years ago the provinces of Japan were under great barons, or daimiyos, who in turn were under the Shogun, the political ruler of the country. The Shogun indeed acknowledged the Mikado as the supreme ruler of Dai Nippon, but nevertheless kept him shut up in Kiyoto in absolute seclusion, as a deity whom it would be blasphemous even so much as to look upon. So the people knew little of the Mikado except as an invisible god. They knew the Shogun was the real ruler, though they never saw him either, for when he travelled along any street or any road the advance guard closed all houses, ordered everyone to go within and bow to the ground, and forbade so much as peeping. The retainers would have cut down anyone whom they had so much as suspected of looking out. Shoguns had ruled as Mayors of the Palace, and Prime Ministers and Generalissimos, since the middle of the twelfth century, but an historian discovered that formerly the Mikado had ruled actually as well as theoretically. This, with the rise of Shintoism, the ancient mythological cult of Japan, jealousy of the Tokugawa family, who held the Shogunate from 1603 to 1867, and the arrival of the foreigners who came in after Commodore Perry had made a treaty with the Shogun in 1854, brought about a revolution which ended in the disappearance of the Shoguns for good and all, and the reappearance of the Mikado after an invisibility of seven centuries.

When, so to speak, the Japanese was in a baby carriage himself, he developed this device for infants into the jin-riki-sha, which has now come to be the ordinary means of locomotion in the chief cities of the Far East, in China, Straits Settlements, India, and even Africa. He has taught the whole world decoration. Wherever one goes now, Japanese art is in evidence. How innumerable are the homes it has helped to beautify! Professor Chamberlain says: "In the days before Japanese art became known to Europe, people then used to consider it essential to

IN THE KINDERGARTEN DAYS

have the patterns on plates, cushions, and what not, arranged with geometrical accuracy. If on the right hand there was a Cupid looking to the left, then on the left hand there must be a Cupid of exactly the same size looking to the right, and the chief feature of the design was invariably in the exact centre. The Japanese artisan artists have shown us that this mechanical symmetry does not make for beauty. They have taught us the charm of irregularity, and if the world owe them but this one lesson, Japan may yet be proud of what she has accomplished."

Not only are the Japanese proficient in diplomacy and in statecraft, but they have great scientific attainments too. They lead the world far and away in biology. They are in the very first rank of chemists, and their schools have some features that other seats of learning lack. There is, for instance, in the "Dai Gakko," or Imperial University, in Tokio, a Chair of Seismology and a Chair of Sanitary Engineering. They have some of the largest battleships afloat; an army that is *ready* the moment it is needed, with the best commissariat and hospital corps the world has ever seen; and, to crown all, England and Japan now are partners.

NOTE.—A friend calls my attention to one of New Japan's first attempts to be like (!) Europeans. On the introduction of telegraphy, she wished to cut down the magnificent rows of Cryptomeria that are the glory of the ancient roadways, and to put up in their stead telegraph poles.

CHAPTER XXIII

IN TRADE

IT was odd to us that the "shraff" should be invariably Chinese, but he was. Whenever we had occasion to call at a foreign counting-house in Yokohama, Nagasaki, Kobe, or wherever it might be, the man that counted the money was a long-queued Celestial in flowing robes, never a short-haired, frock-coated subject of the Mikado. And this in Japan!—where the natives had held all China in contempt until they whipped her so soundly and speedily that the contempt changed into pity!

"Why is it?" asked Gardner. "Can't Japanese count?"

Okashi said they could count well enough, but that Japanese gentlemen (samurai like himself) abhorred the touch of money, and no other class could be trusted to count it honestly.

We knew that our precious landlord's dislike of the medium of exchange would not allow money to remain near him if there were any possible way of getting rid of it, but we did not know that he could count. There was truth in what he said, however. His statement merely lacked comprehensiveness.

When Gardner asked an English friend about the shraffs, the man replied—

"Yes, we have the Chinaman every time, if we can get him. We can trust him. We can't trust the natives. We have tried them and it doesn't do. Come over to the go-downs and I'll show you something.

"There," he said, when we had reached the warehouses, "those three buildings are half-full of stuff one or other of us has got from home, on positive orders. They would be full up, if we had not given a lot of machinery away to make room for other goods that had to come in out of the rain. The men who gave us the orders are among the richest merchants in Yokohama, but while the goods were on the way they changed their minds, or exchange went against them. That left the orders on our hands.

"Now a Chinaman would not have treated us that way. He would take what he had ordered, even if he lost by it, because he would be unwilling to 'lose his face'—that is, his credit.

"When I was first over, a Japanese merchant whom I had met several times pleasantly, and had had some small business dealings with in London, wanted a thousand bolts of flannel. I gave him the price, which he said was satisfactory, and then I cabled for the goods. A few days later he came in and said he wanted a dozen cows. I told him that cows weren't much in my line, but I knew an agent in Seattle who could get him twelve hundred if he wished. We talked over the price he was willing to pay, and incidentally I remarked that I had received word from home that the flannel was on the way.

"'Yes,' he said; 'but now I do not wish flannel; I need cows.'

"'You do not mean cows instead of flannel?'

"'Yes.'

"'But I have ordered the flannel. It is already on the way. It is too late to change.'

"'Probably that may be so,' he replied, 'but as I do not desire the flannel I hope you will obtain cows instead.'

"I did not order cows, but the flannel came promptly enough. I have part of it still. The rest I sold at a loss of 25 per cent. to the very man I had ordered it for in the first place. No one else would touch it. To all that I said to him he only answered, 'Shikataga nai,' which means 'doing way is not,'—or, 'the joke is on you.' It was a good lesson for me, just what I needed to fit me for business over here. Why, my present partner has been here twenty-five years and says he hasn't found a man he can trust yet—that is, among the natives.

"Here's a good instance, right here in your *Things Japanese*. I knew the parties, and Professor Chamberlain has stated the case accurately.

"Kimura is rich. He used to be the manager of the Yokohama Specie Bank. When this happened he was a director, and even now he is President of the Yokohama Guild. So you can see his standing is good. Just let me read you this. It is a fair sample:—

"'May 29, 1894. Messrs. Cornes & Co. of Yokohama, sold to Mr. Kimura Reimon, for delivering in September and October, one hundred bales of yarn, " Purple Hokuroku" quality, but to be marked with a red ticket instead of a purple. On arrival of the goods, Mr. Kimura refused to take delivery on the plea of difference of colour in the ticket. These tickets are the ordinary marks the trade uses in distinguishing grades and qualities. Finding it impossible to get him to make a settlement of any kind, Messrs. Cornes & Co. decided to take the case into court; but, before doing so, they, for reasons peculiar to this country, placed a statement of the dispute before the Yarn Traders' Guild of Yokohama. This body replied that another application should be made to the firm by Mr. Kimura, failing which it would endeavour to bring the two parties together, and, failing that again, the case might be filed. Upon this Mr. Kimura was again approached. He asked for time to consider, and was given until March 10. The reply having been received by March 15, and Messrs. Cornes being anxious to avoid litigation, they requested the personal intervention of three prominent members of the Guild. But Mr. Kimura refused even to discuss the matter with them. The case was at length taken into court.

"'After several hearings, beginning on May 16, before Judge Akiyama and two assistants, judgment was postponed at the request of defendant till July 9. Three days before this term, namely on July 6, the standing committee of the Guild waited on the foreign firm to inform them that unless they agreed to withdraw the suit and accept as a settlement the delivery of thirty-five bales (cancelling the sale of the remaining sixty-five bales) at contract price, and waive all charges, *no dealer would be allowed to call at their office.* Messrs. Cornes declined these terms, but on the following day (July 7) offered to withdraw the suit, provided Mr. Kimura would take delivery of fifty bales at contract price, and pay half interest and fire assurance. These offers the Guild declined. Judgment was delivered on July 9 to the following effect:—

"'Defendant to take delivery of the hundred bales, and to pay the sum of $29,528.59, together with insurance ($837.70), interest ($139.61), and go-down rent ($112), minus ninety days usually allowed pending delivery.'

"'On July 18 a general meeting of the Yokohama Guild was held, with the result that Mr. Kimura's action was fully indorsed, and Messrs. Cornes condemned to a boycott in which the dealers in Tokio, Nagoya, and other important towns were to be asked to join. The next incident was a visit to Messrs. Cornes by representatives of the Tokio Guild, who came to say that they were determined to settle the dispute, and that unless their arbitration were accepted they would join the boycott. Messrs. Cornes having previously ascertained from an eminent Japanese lawyer that Japanese law could afford them no redress, were compelled to accept the Tokio Guild's offer of arbitration, and were thereupon informed that Mr. Kimura would take delivery within sixty days of the hundred bales at $93½ per picul, the foreign firm to pay their own legal expenses. This, which meant a loss of over $2500, had perforce to be submitted to.'

"Now that is the sort of thing that happens every time a foreigner tries to force a native. The native has all the advantage on his side, and he uses it."

"Well, why don't you merchants unite against the Guild—boycott the boycotters?" asked Gardner.

"There are too many kinds of us," was the reply, "and only one kind of native. You can't do much uniting in a community that is Chinese, English, American, German, French, Italian, Portuguese, Dutch, Indian, Parsee, and what not. Even the white foreigners can't keep together. If we were only English and Americans we could accomplish something, but when it comes to getting Frenchmen to stand shoulder to shoulder with Germans—*ausgespielt!*"

We got pretty much the same story from every merchant that we spoke to. Some of them would allow the Japanese merchants no sense of business decency whatever, while others said it was not so much actual dishonesty as total ignorance of the principles of trade, and no idea of the value of credit.

The Japanese, on the other hand, told us that it was not their fault, for they had not enough capital to take great risks or to wait long for things to come from Europe. One man said—

"It is very hard to take things that we do not need. It is not our fault that the foreign merchant has to order things from a long way off. Nor is it our fault if exchange varies. Why should we lose money by such causes? Then, too, when we began to trade with foreigners they sold us many worthless things. We could not judge values of imports in the early days of foreign intercourse. We trusted foreign merchants and they took advantage of our ignorance. Now they are suffering from the bad examples they set us."

It is probably true that those samurai who tried to be merchants after the break up of the feudal system were soon in a bad way. They trusted foreign agents implicitly, with sad results. It was not only the foreigner, however. Merchants of their own race treated them badly. There have been many queer instances of these business methods. Some of them show that a native can "do" another native as complacently as he can do a foreigner. One lager beer brewing company, for instance, which does an enormous business, abstained a long time from paying dividends because it needed the money for bottles which had to be imported. The directors, as individuals, bought the bottles and sold them to the company. The stock-holders paid, and the individual directors pocketed the profits, which quite ate up all chance for dividends. A native told us that the bottle business was very pleasant, the net gain being about 600 per cent.

Another lot of directors who were pretty well under the control of one of the wealthy merchants put up a hat factory under American supervision, and fitted it with the best English machinery. The merchant received £5, 10s. for every £1 he spent for the machinery, — so the superintendent told us. The merchant had the advantage of knowing what machinery was worth, while the stock-holders to whom he sold it had no idea at all. Business was dull on account of the low duty on imported hats, so the merchant made less money than he had hoped. He must devise a plan. What his plan was none except himself knows, but one night the factory burned down.

The fire was a good example of "Tokio no hana," for the whole force of working men and women had a grand picnic by the ruins the next day. There was no limit to the saké and the rice and fish, and other things that Japanese picnickers are fond of. Then the directors ordered a new set of machines from England, and charged the company seven prices instead of five.

Japanese courts recognise the lack of business sense and training on the part of those who appear before them, and deal paternally with the contestants. When a breach of contract comes up for investigation, the interested parties go over the contracts and agreements carefully and explain every item to the best of their ability. Then the court studies the conditions under which the contract would needs be carried out if the contractor should go on with his work. If it finds no obstacle in the way of fulfilment, it decides against the contractor; but if it finds the contractor had miscalculated, and would lose money were he to go on with the work, it decides for him, as manifestly it would be a hardship were he forced to work without profit.

The court communicates with the man who let the contract, saying, "Oki no doku Sama" and "Shikata ga nai" most graciously. Then it suggests that he make a new contract and give the other party a better chance. This is a method of procedure hardly calculated to develop business acumen or the courage that is so often necessary for successful enterprise.

Feudalism had much to do with the disgrace attaching to trade—feudalism and the policy of isolation, which early missionary meddling with Japanese State affairs forced upon the country early in the seventeenth century. The Shogun, Tokugawa Iyeyasu, was in control then. He discovered that the Dominicans and Franciscans had political as well as spiritual ends in view. He believed they were advance agents of Spain and Portugal, and, being adverse to having Japan become the possession of a foreign power, he cleared the country of Christians, though only after furious persecutions, and then shut it up. One Dutch ship a year visited Nagasaki, and that was the extent of Japan's foreign intercourse until Commodore Perry's arrival in 1853.

During these years, whatever Japan may have known of foreign business ways she naturally forgot, while at the same time the class organisation of society continued. The feudal idea was that the only honourable men, except scholars and some priests, were military. The merchant was at the foot of the social ladder. He had almost no rights at all. Politically he was a cipher. He did not venture to call his life his own. His wit and his cunning were all he could depend upon. If he had a dispute with samurai, and the samurai cut him down, there would be one less merchant for the next census to report;

the law would not call a member of the military class to account for trying his sword on a mere tradesman; and anyway merchants should be patient and respectful. So it was that society having denied honour to merchants for many centuries, its possession became valueless, and appreciation of it disappeared.

Now, however, there is a serious attempt at improvement, as we learned in talking to one of the leading men in the Japanese Consular service. Gardner had quoted the Cornes-Kimura incident, and the Consul had deplored the conditions that made such a thing possible.

"We are working hard," he said, "to show merchants the value of credit. I think the fact that the Chinese have good credit is rather shaming our folk into better methods. I sometimes quote to them what one of the Hongkong and Shanghai Banking Corporation's managers said in favour of the Chinese. He puts them quite at the top of the list of those who are trustworthy. He told me that in the Shanghai Bank the business with Chinese in twenty-five years amounted to over £32,000,000, and that there had never been a defalcation, so far as he knew. I show our merchants how much more business they would do if they had credit, and I make a point of having the Japanese merchants abroad give data from time to time to illustrate foreign business methods. Besides this, the Minister of Agriculture and Commerce is sending out "Jitsu Renshiu Sei," or practical trade students, whose business it is to study markets all over the world, and report to the various Chambers of Commerce in Japan. These students are under the consuls in various parts of the world, and really supplement their work.

"This has helped us to develop our manufactures on paying lines, and has already increased the nation's wealth. With every recommendation from these sources the Minister has coupled the strongest possible plea for fair and honourable commercial dealing, and the various Chambers are awaking to the fact that credit is a most desirable asset."

NOTE.—One of the foreign countries represented by a minister in Tokio lost prestige with the Japanese, because, when the minister's period of service had expired and his diplomatic career was at an end, he engaged in a commercial enterprise. A Japanese minister could have done this without loss of esteem, for the Japanese would say that his motive was a patriotic desire to develop the resources of his country. But the minister in question being a foreigner, it was said that he did as he did not for his country's sake but for personal reasons, and was therefore selfish.

CHAPTER XXIV

DIVING BELLES

IT is odd that in a country where woman counts for so little there should be some households in which she rules supreme. There are such in the province of Shima, and we found others on the west coast.

"Our New Woman would faint with envy if she could see the way some of her Japanese sisters run things in their homes," said Gardner in one of his discourses. He was talking to some globe-trotters at the Club Hotel one day. "She would realise that with all her bloomers, cigarettes, canes, and masculine shirt fronts, she is yet so far from her goal that she could hardly hope to reach it in this life. She'd either quit living or come to Japan.

"Yes, I know it sounds a little strange. Mrs. Hugh Fraser, Sir Edwin Arnold, and Lafcadio Hearn say that the Japanese woman is the gentlest person in the world, and that she is as sweet and charming as she is mild. Sir Edwin Arnold writes about the 'three obediences'—'As a child she obeys her father, as a wife she obeys her husband, and as a mother she obeys her eldest son.' That's true of almost all the women, but had Sir Edwin been with us he might have seen something to make another story out of.

"I first heard of the Japanese New Woman, who, by the way, isn't at all new, when I was over in Noto, that little peninsula on the west coast that juts up into the Japan Sea.

"I had been knocking about there for a couple of months, and had lost my identity as a foreigner altogether and turned so brown that I was sure I'd never bleach out again. I lived in a temple; and that is a point to remember if you roam off the beaten tracks in Japan. Temples are better than hotels. The priests I lived with were of the Hongwanji sect. They had wives, and their wives could cook. Board and lodging cost me twelve shillings a month. I never saw the country inn that could do better.

"Worshippers from every part of Noto came to this temple, for it was older than any man could say, and famous. Through the good offices of these priests I made friends in many conditions of life. The folk I grew most interested in were some fisherwomen who came from a cluster of tiny hamlets down the coast. In travelling by the hill-roads one wouldn't see a sign of this hamlet, although one might be only a stone's-throw away. This was because it was hidden under the cliff.

"I noticed these women at the temple several times, but there were never any men with them. Women from other places came with their husbands. These women didn't, but they had children who called them 'mama,' so I knew there must be husbands somewhere. They were handsome, with clear skin, bright eyes, and rounded limbs which their peasant garb scarcely at all concealed. I couldn't understand why there were no men with them.

"One evening as my best friend among the priests sat with me, enjoying a feast the inhabitants offered up that day to the astral body of the dead headsman of the village, I learned the reason. My friend was born in one of those hamlets, and would have been there yet if his mother hadn't said that he should be a priest. His mother, mind you, not his father. That sounded strange, for I had been in the country so long that I had forgotten that women ever expressed an opinion.

"'Yes,' my friend went on, as he rubbed his hand over his shaven poll, 'it was fortunate for me, because a man doesn't have a good time down there. He has to stay in the house to do the cooking and to keep things clean. That is because he can't swim. At least, he can't swim as well as a woman. Why, my mother can swim two days in the busy season and not be used up, but my father would be tired out if he stayed in the water six hours.

"'That's the way the women earn a living,' added the priest. 'If none of the people could swim they would have to go somewhere else, for there is no other work to do there. These shell-fish that you like so well,' he said, picking up a portion of the offering to the august departed, 'come from there. They are difficult to get. The women go down twenty-five to fifty feet after them. While the woman is diving for shell-fish the man is at home caring for the house. That's the custom in every household.

"'Once I remember a man got drunk, and did not have the dinner ready when his wife came up. She told her friends, and they pulled him into the sea. Then they sat on him, and pushed him down till he was almost drowned. He was crying " Go men nasai" all the time. He wept, and the women laughed—all except his wife. She struck his head with her hand, and called him "dara," which means "lacking" or stupid. When they brought him to the beach again the intoxication was all gone, and he was humble.

"'People in Japan generally do not know about this place,' continued my friend; 'a foreigner never saw it.

"'One day when I was a small boy I went with my mother to sell shell-fish on Kashima. When we were there a ship anchored off the shore. A boat full of men with green eyes and white clothes came to land. They took my mother's shell-fish and all the pickles on the island. Then they went away. Someone said they were "Rokoku no hito" (Russians). I don't know, but they are the only foreigners most of us have ever seen.'

"'Does your mother ever come here?' I asked.

"'Oh yes; she is coming to-morrow, and I am going back with her. Wouldn't you like to go too? If you would condescend to travel in such rude company, and to enter our unworthy hovel, we shall be honoured greatly.'

"'I should be very glad indeed,' I said. It was quite too good a chance to lose.

"The next day his mother came. He said she was his mother, though she did not look to be thirty years old. She was plump and graceful and merry. On her back was a boy, her grandson as I learned afterwards, just past his sixth birthday. She had carried him sixteen miles that morning. When she had bowed to us a half-dozen times she took a dip in the sea, gliding through the water like a seal, and then entered the temple.

"Then we all seated ourselves in the guest-room, and she nursed the six-year-old at her breast. (Grandmothers do that here in Japan.)

"She was going back that afternoon," she said.

"'It will be moonlight, and we can be there by ten o'clock,' she explained. 'I do not like to leave the husband there all alone.'

"I flattered her a little, and when dinner was served offered her my saké cup so often with my profoundest bow that she said she would wait till morning.

"She woke us about four o'clock, and by five we were on our way, she carrying the child.

"Before noon we were in her home. The tide was out, so we did not see the women, who were in the water, and were hidden from view beyond some rocks. The men were at home doing chores in a shy, submissive way. Some were preparing shell-fish and laying them on the sandy beach to dry, while others were grinding buckwheat flour, of which they would make "soba," the native substitute for macaroni. Some were bringing in faggots, and were putting in order the square holes that in every peasant's hut serve as fireplace, or were burnishing kettles and doing other odd jobs. No wonder my friend was glad he was a priest.

"With the rising of the tide the women came up. Even the oldest were good-looking. They had pouches hung to belts about their loins, and in these they placed the shell-fish they found upon the bottom. All of the pouches had something in them, many of them were full. As each one came out she emptied her pouch into a common pile on the beach, and one of the older women called off the name from a book, and made a mark opposite. The marks seemed all alike, so I suppose the women were communists. The priest told me that all the villagers were in one company, and that each member did the best she could for the good of all. If anyone grew lazy there was a penalty, but it had not been used for so long he had forgotten what it was.

"As I stood watching the heap grow, the priest's father came to us, and bowing low, said, 'Honourable pardon deign! There is absolutely nothing either to eat or to drink, but please honourably condescend to partake.'

"I followed him into the house, and was just sitting down to a banquet of many shapes and sizes, the like of which I had never seen before, when there was a commotion outside.

"'Nan deshoka!' exclaimed the priest. 'What's up?' 'Ah, korario' (come here). I hurried after him. There was a luckless man in the midst of a mob of women. He was protesting, and they, talking all at once, were heading to the sea, just like the case of which my friend had told me. The man was ducked, and then laid out to dry.

"'Was he drunk?' I asked. 'Oh no. That woman

in the tub over there fell in love with him, and his wife found them talking together this morning. Now she is telling him that he must not have eyes or ears for other women. He will be careful after this, for he doesn't like the sea.'

"The woman in the tub was burnishing her arms with a small bag of rice powder, and paid little attention to what was going on. No one said anything to her, though she was the cause of the trouble.

"I wonder what will happen when the shell-fish become extinct?"

CHAPTER XXV

AMONGST THE GODS

LIVING in the temples, as we did during the greater part of the time we were in Japan, we grew familiar with the images of the saints and heroes and the gods and goddesses whom the temples honour. This familiarity did not breed contempt, but gave us a personal interest and a feeling akin to reverence. Certainly we could reverence some of the ideas for which, in Buddhist minds, those strange images stood. The gods had their humorous side, too.

When pious Japanese are ill they rub Binzuru. If they are very ill, they ask the priests to hang a bib about his neck or to put a cap on him and mitts. Binzuru is the head of the great faith-cure of Japan; a sort of Buddhist science, like the so-called Christian science of America, of which, indeed, it might have been anciently the prototype, though the rubbers do not call their rubbing "science." But it is fully equal scientifically to the orisons of the ogygian healers on the other side of the Pacific, and its efficacy is similar.

Binzuru shows the effect of so great faith. His nose is gone and his abdomen, his kneecaps also, and there is a great hollow in his chest. The process of

GOKU TEMPLE

his wearing out—or rather in—does not worry him, however. What matters it if all his organs go, so long as his disciples rescue theirs from the ravages of disease? And, besides, the simple faith of those who believe in him is agreeable to his contemplation. Therein is his reward.

The story goes that this far-famed healer, whose image is ubiquitous in Japan, was one of the sixteen Rakkan once, that is one of the perfected saints whom Buddha chose for his immediate disciples; but he backslid a little in a way that shows that early Buddhism looked upon the female sex much as did early Christianity centuries afterwards: he noticed one day that a woman was beautiful, and said so in the hearing of another perfected saint, who straightway reported him to the Master. Buddha put poor Binzuru down a full hair's-breadth in the scale of virtue, but to offset this punishment gave him power to cure all human ills.

Generally in Buddhist temples Binzuru sits outside the chancel because of his unfortunate remark, but he is all the easier of access for this reason, and is probably as popular as Jizo, the patron saint of children and of travellers. He has small opportunity for loneliness unless he wakes up of nights, for rubbers are about him from the first opening of the temple doors until their closing. Even at night some say the holy images commune together. If this is so, what a wondrous tale the pigeon-hunting owl might tell of what he sees as he looks in upon the sacred precincts on his rounds.

One finds Binzuru in temples of all degrees of

wealth, and of many sects. He is on good terms with the Kami or Shinto gods and the Hotoke or Buddhist deities. He is more often in the "tera," or Buddhist temple, however, than in the "miya," the Shinto temple, for Buddhism is the popular religion of Japan and receives the Shinto gods into its pantheon with cordial welcome. So in looking for the Healer, the man with faith and a pain he would be rid of, does not look with much expectancy beyond the gateway of the miya, in shape like that of the Greek π, but goes through the tera's gate with confidence.

We watched a man one day as he approached Binzuru in all humility and childlike faith. How gently, almost caressingly, he runs his hand along the Healer's side and then up and down his own! He was badly bent when he came in, but he walked away erect and grateful. For him Binzuru is far better than a plaster. Just by the man stood a woman. She was well, but the infant in her arms had trouble with its eyes. So the mother stroked the image's old worn face, her hand scarce hiding more than half its eye, and then touched the baby lids, saying, "Namu Amida Butsu" ("Behold Amida the Buddha"). It reminds one of Lourdes.

Amida is Boundless Light. He and Binzuru are great friends. His image is not far away. His "goku," or halo, is widespread, typical of his radiance. Sometimes it is like a great oval screen of gold behind him, but his almost certain sign for recognition is the position of his hands lying in his lap, the fingers crossed and the thumb tips barely touching.

THE TERA OR BUDDHIST TEMPLE

AMONGST THE GODS

On the other side, so near that the babe's wee hand touched him as the mother passed with her infant cooing now, is Daruma the Abstracted, or, as some say, "legless," who lost himself in contemplation of the Infinite fourteen centuries ago, and withered slowly as he sat until his nether limbs dropped off. Looking at his features, one fancies that this contemplation is still in progress, and that it will continue until all beings are united into the Eternal Absolute.

It is Daruma, by the way, whom legend credits with the origin of tea. Before he went off into his present trance he had made another effort at permanent contemplation, and had failed through falling asleep at the end of the ninth year. When he awoke he was so vexed at his eyelids for their drooping that he cut them off. No sooner had they fallen to the ground than, lo! they took root, sprouted, and sent forth leaves. As the old monk looked in wonder, a disciple of the Buddha appeared and told him to brew the leaves of the new shrub and then drink thereof. Daruma plucked the leaves, which now all the world knows as tea, did as the vision commanded him to do, and has not slept a moment since.

The "Heavenly Shiner" is over opposite the Daruma. Ama-Terasu is her name. She is a most important personage in Japan, for she was the mother of the first Mikado. One of her images is so sacred that only the holiest of priests and personages of Imperial blood may look into the room where it is kept. The image itself no one ever sees. It is wrapped in a silken sack, in a box of chamæcyparis wood, which rests on a stand under a white silk cloth. For centuries this box was the special charge of a virgin daughter of the Mikado. Even she never saw the sacred relic, for as age began to tell upon the silken sack she put a new sack on over the old one without undoing it. Before she did this, she had to fast three days, to bathe three times each day, and during the ceremony to wear garments of material fresh from the loom—garments that no one had ever worn nor would ever wear again.

A Minister of State lost his life for being curious as to the appearance of the apartment wherein the image of this Imperial ancestor reposes. He pushed aside an intervening curtain with his cane, and peeped. A young Government clerk in Tokio, Nishino by name, hearing of this peep some months later, went to Ise, to Goku Temple, the scene of the sacrilege, to confirm the story. Then he returned to Tokio and stabbed the Minister with a kitchen fish-knife, so that he died. This was Viscount Mori, who had been Minister Plenipotentiary to Washington and to London, and at the time of his death was in the Imperial Cabinet as head of the Department of Education.

As affording a glimpse into the Japanese mind, it is interesting to note that popular sympathy was altogether with the murderer, whom an officer of the Minister's household cut down, striking off his head with a single blow of his sabre. The newspapers abused this officer, but not a word for the Viscount nor for his family, whom Nishino's act had plunged into grief on the greatest gala day of Japan's history.

THE GATEWAY OF THE MIYA, SHINTO TEMPLE

It was February 11, 1889, the day on which the Mikado presented a Constitution to his people.

The young fanatic's grave in the Yanaka cemetery became sacred as though it were a saint's. There was a great pyramid of wreaths on it, which daily pilgrimages replenished till at last the Government had to interfere and forbid all ceremonies there except by relatives. The assassin is now to all intents and purposes a saint, for though this happened twelve years ago natives still pray to Nishino to intercede for them with Heaven on their behalf.

The priests at Ise tell you that Ama-Terasu was born from the left eye of Izanagi, the Creator, just after a visit to Hades, where he had been to see his wife. Ama had trouble with her brother, the Impetuous Male, Susa-no-o, who was born of Izanagi's right eye. In her vexation she hid herself in a cavern, which was a thoughtless thing for a sun-goddess to do as it made the whole world dark. The other gods and goddesses came to the cavern's mouth to coax Ama-Terasu out. Ama would not come. Then they danced and sang, and the sun-goddess ventured just to peep, when one of the gods held up a mirror, and catching sight of the reflection of her own lovely face Ama-Terasu came out and the universe had light once more.

Not far away from the sun-goddess is an eight-armed image of Marishiten, whom in India folks call Krishna. She lives in Ursa Major, whence she oversees the sun and the moon, using two of her arms in guiding them.

Within speaking distance sits a sweet-faced image

whose lap is full of children's tokens, dolls and bibs and little caps, the offerings of mothers whose children the gods have called. She is Kishi Bojin, Protectress of Children. Often she speaks of her miraculous conversion. Like St. Paul, she changed from an enemy into the friend of a new religion. She had determined to destroy the Buddhists, "being exceedingly mad against them." But she turned into a dragon, and gave birth to five hundred children whom Heaven decreed she should eat—at the rate of one each day.

Gautama, the Buddha, taking pity, restored her to womanhood and taught her the Doctrine, whereupon she entered a convent, and ever since has been the protectress of those whom formerly she would destroy. She holds a pomegranate in one hand, which emblem is her crest.

Just over Kojin, the Kitchen god, whom the housewife looks well after, are the Sam-biki-Zaru, or three monkey gods. Saru means monkey. In combination with other words it is pronounced Zaru. One of these gods of the prehensile tail has his hands over his mouth, he is the Iwa Zaru or Dumb Monkey god; another stops his ears, he is the Kita Zaru, Deaf Monkey god; and the third covers his eyes, he is Mi-Zaru, the Blind Monkey god: a good trinity these, for they refuse to speak evil, to look upon it, or to listen to it. Mrs. Grundy does not stand well with them.

There is an image of Kompira also, who has especial care of those who go down into the sea in ships. Some call him Kotohira. For centuries he

AMONGST THE GODS

was a Buddhist pure and simple, and at one time so eager was he to bring mankind to the true faith that he took on the form of a crocodile with a body one thousand feet long, possessed of one thousand heads and one thousand arms. Thus arrayed he made many converts. There was a grand Buddhist temple in his honour at the foot of Zozu San Shikoku until recently. It dated back nearly twelve centuries. Thirty years ago the Shintoists came into power for a little, and claimed this temple, saying that Kompira belonged to them for they had worshipped him since the world began. So the Government let them have their way. They tore down nearly all of the ancient tera and put a miya in its place. But the people throng there regularly on the tenth and eleventh days of October each year, just as they did anciently, for whether Kompira is Buddhist or Shinto is a small matter in their eyes; they love him for himself alone.

Monkeys are not the only animals natives reverence in Japan. There are pink-eyed horses, alive and fat, within their sacred stalls just inside the temple gates. Those who desire grace give these pink-eyed ones a shell full of beans, which the attending Doctor of Divinity supplies at a ha'penny a shell. Besides the horses there are stone foxes, Imari, goddesses of the fruitful rice-fields. Farmers' wives decorate these images with bibs, and then if the good women have faith, proper seed, sufficient water, and good fertilisers, they may expect crops.

Another acquaintance of Binzuru's is the god of Wisdom, Fudo, whose throne appears to be on fire.

Apparently his wisdom has not made him happy, for his countenance is anything but joyous. He is armed with a sword in his right hand and a lariat in the other. It is rumoured that he ropes in the wicked and despatches them. Emma O, sitting opposite, glares quite as fiercely as Awful Wisdom. He is regent of the Buddhist hells, and receives all-comers according to their deserts. His attending scribe and reader have kept a record of each soul. The record is true, and there is no escape from the sentence that Emma O pronounces. Tradition says that the regent was a great Chinese general, whose love of truth exceeded every other love, so that he turned his back upon the throne of the Heavenly Kingdom when his legions offered it to him, sought out one whom he believed should have it by right of birth, established him, and then retired to the obscurity of private life. However this may be, Emma O is the patron of many a joss-house the world over, and it is before his image that Chinese administer their most sacred oaths and make compacts binding by chopping off the heads of cocks.

Despite the furious faces of Fudo and Emma O there is no fear upon the countenances of the seven gods of Luck, the Shichi Fukujin, whom Binzuru looked kindly on before his eyes were rubbed away. There is the Honest Labour god, Ebisu the fisherman, whose name all drinkers of good beer in Japan must be familiar with. He has just caught a noble bream, a fish the Japanese call "tai." Next to him is Daikoku with his bales of rice. He is richer than a Trust. The Tokio folk are laying out a pleasure park in his

AMIDA, THE BUDDHA

honour, with a grand Daikoku statue, malet and rice bales included, in the midst thereof. Benten is a lady, and is musical. She can charm snakes, and uses one to go about with instead of a motor-car. Fukurokuji has a long head, and a pet crane with a neck almost as long. Both he and his pet signify longevity. Bishamon, with his spear and Pagoda, in protective armour like unto a battle-ship, is the lucky god of War. Jurokujin has the great good fortune to know the thoughts of animals. They come to him in perfect trust, for friendship's sake. No menagerie should be without Jorokujin. Singularly enough, Hotei, the seventh god of Luck, who is supposed to represent good-nature, is stout, one might say fat, and has a high sack of sustenance to lean back against.

Of course there are many Shakas in this temple of gods—images of Gautama, the Buddha, to whom existence as he had known it in Far Eastern countries was a weariness. Where he journeyed to and fro, human vitality was at low ebb and life a constant struggle. He sought escape therefrom, and found it in the knowledge which contemplation and pure living give. Having conquered all desire, the illusions of the world revealed themselves to him and he was ready for Nirvana, but he declined to enter until he had shown the truth to every other living creature and they too had become worthy of the great reward. When the others were safely in he would follow after.

The goddess of Mercy has many images, too. Her name is Kwannon. She possesses the omnipotent gem " nyo-i-rin," and has the Twenty-eight Constellations to wait on her. Professor Chamberlain likes Kwannon, and knows all about her thousand arms, her horse's head, her eleven faces, and her wondrous gem, as well as about the " Saikoku Sanju-san Sho," or Thirty-Three Shrines, sacred to her. They are all near Kiyoto. This is what the Professor discovered as to their origin—

Many years ago lived a famous Buddhist Abbot, Tokudo Shonin by name. Suddenly, as the Japanese say of holy men, he "divinely retired"—that is, he died. He went to the Underworld, where two dignitaries from the court of the regent Emma O met him with respectful salutations, and conducted him with much ceremony to the August Presence.

"I have sent for your Holiness," said Emma O, "because I know from the piety of your life that I may trust you even as your children upon earth have learned to trust you. I have an important mission for you."

Then he told the Abbot of thirty-five places the goddess of Mercy was interested in particularly, and of her labours to save the world. In her great love for mankind she had divided herself into three-and-thirty parts or bodies, and each of these bodies had become the guardian spirit of one of the Thirty-Three Holy Places; each Place having power to cure one of the spiritual ills that flesh is heir to.

"At present," said Emma O, "the men and the women of the world above do not know of the existence of these Places. They do evil instead of good, and come dropping into hell as rain falls in a sudden summer shower. It shall be your work to inform them how they may avoid this horrid fate. Tell them to make pilgrimages to the Three-and-Thirty Holy Places, and then, having worshipped at them all, they shall radiate light even from the soles of their feet and shall have power to crush all the hells there ever were. So sure am I of this that should one that has made this pilgrimage backslide, I myself will suffer in his stead. Here is my seal to take up with you as a testimony of the authority of the message which you bear."

Now while Tokudo had been in hell his body had lain in the Abbey three days and three nights, the priests thinking he might return, as the body did not grow cold. At the beginning of the fourth day the Abbot awoke with the seal in his hand as testimony. Immediately he and his followers visited the Places, erected shrines, and the downpour of souls into hell diminished.

CHAPTER XXVI

ON THE EARTHQUAKE PLAN

WE were up to dine near the Imperial University in Tokio one evening, in the beautiful puzzle-pathed grounds known as Kaga Yashiki, where once the Prince of Kaga had his palace. The house in which we met was long and low, all but the central part, which had been the Government Observatory in the early days of the University. The telescopes had gone, however, and instead of being a place for the study of the movements of other worlds, the building had become one for the investigation of movements nearer home—an earthquake laboratory, as it were, where these uncanny disturbances made records on the various contrivances a famous specialist had devised for measuring all sorts of jolts and jars and palpitations. Their capacity for notation included all disturbances, from the upheaval of a mountain range to the alighting of the most careful fly.

Naturally the conversation took the earthquake turn, and the Professor, our host, whose home was in the building, had many interesting things to tell us on the subject of seismology. He explained

ON THE EARTHQUAKE PLAN

what a "quake" did to an earth particle during a seismic disturbance, how it moved east and west, north, south, and up and down. He showed a "track" a colleague of his, Professor Sekiya, had made to illustrate the movement. The track was of wire, bent and wound and turned about, in and out, till it looked like a skein of yarn a kitten had been playing with. To follow it from end to end would have taken a patient man a week. But it was accurate undoubtedly, for the Professor and his assistants had worked it out from thousands of seismograph records which they had collected from many parts of the world. The seismograph told the truth, the Professor declared, for he had tested it on stands he had built especially for artificial oscillation. The record of the seismographs and the known oscillation of the stands corresponded exactly.

It was wonderful, especially to those of us who were "griffins."

"O for an earthquake!" said the griffins.

"Well, you may not have long to wait," said the Professor. "We have about five hundred a year in Japan, you know. One may be along before the evening's over."

And he spoke truly, for the servants had no more than brought on the fish when the floor began to wriggle, the lamps and pictures to sway, the windows to rattle, and the dishes on the mahogany to clatter about like a lot of frightened turtles.

The Professor had just made a remark about earthquakes' construction when the swirling began.

He looked round at us as though to observe individual effects, and said—

"Here you are, boys. How singularly *a propos*. I'll have some good records to show you in the morning. Meanwhile, as this building is a bit old, I suggest we get under the table. It is built on the earthquake plan, and should the roof fall we are safe there."

By the time he had said "there" all of us were there, riding on the sea-less billows of the floor, which creaked and undulated and bumped our heads against the table's under surface, and rolled us against its stalwart legs, and against each other, as though we were great dough billiard-balls trying to make cannon and cushion shots. These were the sensations, as I can testify after comparing notes with my companions, but as none of us had on seismographs I cannot say that I am dynamically correct.

When we came out from under the table the fish was cold, but we had had such a warm time we did not mind. We told the Professor that he was the cleverest arranger we had ever known. We had never met before with such a happy combination of theory and practice, and we all said—

"Here's looking at you."

It was excellent sherry, an additional reason for not caring that the fish was cold.

The Professor lighted a cigarette, and as the entrée came on smiled and said—

"Thank you kindly, but really it's only this— anyone must see that a good strong table like this may be a protection if one is on the right side of it—the under side, for instance; and as to the earthquake coming along just as we were talking—that is not so extraordinary. Quite often my friends mention earthquakes when they are up here, and in a country where there are fifty-one volcanoes it would be strange if a quake did not come opportunely at times. Upheavals and subsidences are going on all the time. All Japan is an upheaval; and off the coast a bit, say from fifty to two hundred miles east of Sendai, a town north of here, there is one of the greatest depressions in the world's crust we know of: the Tuscarera Deep we call it, after the United States Government vessel that discovered it. It would be safe to dive from the top of Fuji into Tuscarera Deep—at least there would be plenty of water and no danger of striking bottom. The depth is over 24,000 feet—Fuji, the highest point of Japan's upheaval, is 12,400 feet, so we have 36,000 feet between top and bottom; a safe seven miles, I fancy."

"Do you think, Professor," asked one of the party, "that old Tuscarera dropped a mile or so just now, or did Fuji shoot up farther into the sky?"

"Oh no. Neither. This was just a bit of a rumble down Yokohama way, nearly twenty miles off, where the centre of disturbance is for this particular region. I daresay we'll have a recurrence, and to-morrow we'll read in the papers, when they come up from Yokohama, that some chimneys are over. It was lively enough to do that."

Again the Professor spoke truly. The recurrence came, and with its coming we went below as before, and listened to the ballet of the dishes overhead. We did not stay as long this time, however; and when a third shock came we were down for just a moment, and then only from force of habit. We believed in the Professor's scheme, however, and each of us decided to have a heavy table round somewhere so long as we had residence in the country.

"Another point for you chaps that live in foreign style," said the Professor, "and one to remember, is that a heavy bedstead is a good thing. If a quake comes after you have retired, roll out and under, and there you are safe though the heavens fall. If any of you build here, see to the door-posts, and especially to the lintels across the tops of the posts. Have the lintels over the windows strong, too, or else do not have the windows directly one above the other. A row of windows running up a wall in a straight line is like the holes in a sheet of postage-stamps. When the quake comes, there's where the wall will tear, right up and down along that row of windows."

We all agreed to follow the Professor's advice faithfully. Personally I can say that I have never put up walls since that in the least suggested postage-stamp construction. The Professor gave us some further tips, too, which some of us found of great value later on. One man, a Japanese professor, Kashikoi by name, built a house in Yokohama strictly in accordance with the Professor's instructions. He also dug a trench round the border of his grounds about six feet deep, similar to the one round the Engineering College at Kaga Yashiki. The Professor had explained to him how this ditch cut off surface vibrations. These vibrations, it seems, skim along like ripples on the surface of a pond into which a boy has thrown a stone thinking he could hit a frog. A few feet down, the effect of this kind of vibration is practically *nil*. The frame of Kashikoi's house was like a broad inverted V. A neighbour asked him one day if his house was to be all roof.

"No," Kashikoi replied; "but yours will be one of these days, Aho, old chap, if you don't do as I do." And indeed Aho's roof did settle down upon him one night, so close to the ground that it took an hour for his apprehensive friends to dig him out. It was only the shape of the roof, an inverted V, that saved him. Kashikoi, taking advantage of the Professor's experience, shunned a cubic frame like Aho's, which could twist to pieces easily, and he did not have a house all roof either. Only the upper half of the frame was roof. Along the lower half on each side he ran a porch. The frame of the porch looked like wings on the V. The house was between two porches, and as thoroughly protected by the roof-like frame as Aho had been, only much more comfortably.

Kashikoi became expert in chimneys, too, after his first failure. He had an interest in the Yokohama electric light plant, and had let a young Japanese engineer put up the chimney. With the first quake it fell in a heap and smashed things. Examination showed that each brick had fallen separately, what little cement there was between them being of no use at all. Kashikoi had the young engineer up before a committee of investigation. Question followed question, until the young native, seeing no escape, said he had built the thing with non-cohesive cement purposely. Had he used the A1 article the chimney, instead of sinking into a heap in a comparatively small area, would have fallen in a rigid mass extending far from its base and resulting possibly in the death of unsuspecting passers-by.

Chimney number two went up under Kashikoi's personal supervision, large at the base, knitted together with steel bands within the brickwork, and A1 cement throughout.

But to go on with our dinner. Over the coffee and cigarettes our host told of his volcanic experiences, of climbing miles into the air and looking down into boiling craters, and other weird tales. His journeyings are the most comprehensive ever made in Japan. Down near Nagasaki, the chief seaport on the island of Kiushiu, he found the largest active volcano in the world, Aso San; yet, in spite of its activity and the terrible eruptions it has had, there are some seventy villages inside the crater, with a total population of perhaps 20,000. During one eruption Aso San destroyed 50,000 lives— literally obliterated them.

All conditions of men, from the Mikado down to the most lowly, have made offerings and prayers to propitiate the wrath of this vast volcanic mountain. Once, says the Professor, the people heard rumblings

THE EFFECTS OF AN EARTHQUAKE

ON THE EARTHQUAKE PLAN

and went to the priest with money, but in vain—the rumblings continued and the priest said that God probably wanted more money. Then the people gave again, but still God did not grant their prayer. "He thinks you have given insufficiently," explained the priest; so the people gave a third time. Then the holy man beat his sacred drum and clanged the sacred gong, repeated seven prayers, and informed his parishioners that God advised them twice. First, in case of flood run to the hills. Second, in case of earthquakes to run to the bamboo forest, where the matted roots form a network that would hold them up even though the ground should open. And the people went away dissatisfied, for they had known these things all along.

Then the Professor told us of the most extraordinary earthquake phenomena he had ever observed. It had to do with the very table we had been sitting about. It was temporarily in the house of another man then, while the Professor's present house was being put in order for his moving in from another part of the city. There had been a dinner, much like the one to-night, said our host, and after the dinner a little game with a kitty. It was a quiet little game, of the sort that relieves the mind of all sorts of worry, and is restful. Relief indeed comes to anyone sooner or later if he will stick to it. It is one of the game's strong points.

"Well," continued our host, "we had relieved each other quite a bit when one of these quakes came, rather a lively one, and the party disappeared through doors and windows, and under the table, or through the floor, for all I know. When the rumbling ceased, we returned one by one from various retreats, until five of the six were back at the table. We waited for number six, but he did not come; then we searched for half an hour, I should say, until we found him in a wardrobe of the most distant room in the building. He was so upset it took more than was in the soda syphon to restore him. We got him round, however, and resumed our seats at the relief table, but the kitty had disappeared. We never found a trace of it."

CHAPTER XXVII

MISSIONARIES AND MISSIONARIES

WHENEVER our roaming along the byways of Japan brought us to the door of a missionary home we went in and found a welcome. There was always room for two more at the missionary's table, and if we could stay for the night there were always futon enough for a couple of extra beds. This hospitality was due partly, perhaps, to the fact that both he and we were far from home, partly to the genial influence of Japan, where the very atmosphere breathes welcome, but chiefly because the missionary himself was a good fellow—a man living pleasantly and setting a wholesome example.

The example is not exciting, but it is as an example he is most effective. The missionary is taken seriously, as a rule, except when the *Mail*, the *Herald*, or the *Gazette*, being short of copy, gives him opportunity to point out in print the weak spots in the creeds, the customs, the rites or beliefs of his brother missionaries of other sects.

The Japanese smile at him then, and the Buddhists say: "August divergence of august opinion apparently existing is among the teachers of religion from the West." Then they rub their polls and become abstracted in contemplation of absolute unconsciousness. The Imperial Government likes the missionary, and the Mikado decorated one some years ago. Later he and his family were granted all the rights of citizenship. The Minister of State, in transmitting the papers, declared that the Empire was to be congratulated in having so worthy a man within its borders. When this reverend gentleman was presented to the Court of the Heaven - Descended, he gave his Imperial Majesty a Bible, the only one that ever found its way within the palace gates.

Like other folks who accomplish things, the missionary comes in for criticism. He expects this. Sometimes he even welcomes it. As he leaves home to live among the "heathen"—a word, by the way, that he carefully eschews so long as he resides among them — the older women of his church tell him that his noble self-sacrifice awakens pity in their hearts. Pity there is certainly, and admiration, too. These are comforting to him, for to the missionary, as to most folks, it is grievous to give up home.

But after he has lived a year in Japan it would be more grievous were he ordered to return. He has eaten of the lotus. When his seventh year arrives, and he is to come back for a twelvemonth, he does so with some little eagerness to see what home will look like after an absence of six years, and with a joyous expectation of seeing relatives and old friends again; but, after he has seen, his face turns towards the Far

East with yearning, and he is not quite himself again until the land beyond the setting sun—or, as the ancient name describes it, the Land of the Rising Sun—is beneath his feet once more. The Empire he has sought to convert has converted him. He does not say so, perhaps he does not know, but it is a fact.

The missionary is an influential person in the East. He has established schools far and wide, several of them of exceptional excellence. He is the intellectual father of thousands of the young men and women of New Japan. These young folks do not all profess the creed of their teacher, but it is safe to say that not one of them has failed altogether to profit by contact with the foreigner. The young man may still be apt to speak what is not so, probably he is, but at least he has learned there is such a thing as truth-telling—strange and wonderful though it is to him and of doubtful utility—yet worthy of investigation. To accomplish even this is no small gain.

Mission schools teach everything, from chemistry to knitting socks. They represent nearly every denomination of importance in the world, and they dispense knowledge almost without cost. They are a boon to the country, but sometimes the earnest student takes advantage of them, and, if slang may be allowed, he "pulls the missionary's leg."

Such an earnest student soon discovers that he receives more attention from the missionary and from the wife if he shows signs of conversion. Consequently, at whatever school he enters his name, he begins to be converted right away. As he changes from school to school—change being a delight to the Japanese—he is converted frequently. By the time his education is complete he is one of the most converted persons in the world. Indeed, it is not impossible to find a member of the Greek Church who is also a Congregationalist, a French Catholic, a Baptist, a Unitarian, a Methodist, a communicant of the Church of England, and belonging, possibly, to half a dozen minor mission organisations.

The general run of mission students are as religious as the average British youth. Apparently they enjoy their lessons in piety thoroughly, the girls in particular; but they have such gentle natures that it is hard to believe they need instruction in humility and meekness. They are themselves living lessons in these virtues.

The missionary-in-the-cannibal-stew idea is upset by a visit to the houses of the evangelists in Tsukiji, Tokio. One sees there that, even from a worldly point of view, it is not a sad thing to be "called." So long as he is faithful to his creed, he need not worry over worldly matters. His salary will be paid regularly until he resigns or passes on to the land he has sought to prepare so many others for. He will have a home to live in, the mission doctor and pharmacist will attend to him and to his family without charge. He goes to the mountains when the heat of summer comes, usually to Nikko, concerning which place the Japanese legend says: "Nikko wo minai uchi wa kekko to iuna" ("Until you have seen Nikko do not use the word beautiful").

His children may be educated at the mission's expense, and he receives his travelling money for his septennial vacation home.

The salary for bachelor missionaries is about £150 a year, and for married men £300. When one remembers that lodging and medical attendance are found, and that servants' wages are low—cooks, £1 to £1, 10s. a month; nurses and maids, 16s.; and that a jin-riki-sha, with a man to pull it, who finds himself, costs £1 a month—it is not a wonder that the missionary is fairly well content.

Learning the language is the work the missionary takes hold of first. He must master the colloquial, in order to preach to the natives. Usually five years are allowed for this. He may take up the written language, too, if it seems advisable, but no one ever learned that well in five years. It is a large undertaking, for he must learn all over again how to think; the mode of thought and the world of ideas into which he is entering are wholly different from those he was born into.

His teacher shows him that Japanese nouns have neither number nor gender; adjectives, though not compared, have tense and mood inflections. There are no pronouns; verbs do not have person but have a negative voice, and, as Professor Chamberlain says, forms to indicate causation and potentiality. The written language is so different from the spoken that were the daily paper read aloud, a master of the colloquial might not understand even the general import of the article. To read the newspapers comfortably, one should know at least four thousand

Chinese characters. Some minds have given way in the attempt to learn them.

Still, to the missionary with a turn for original investigation, there is an infinite field in Japan, and this has saved men who loved intellectual life, and found little congenial companionship among the natives—history, Buddhism, land tenure, philology, and the intricacies of the native family relationship, are only a few of the subjects that as yet foreigners need light upon. But the missionary is investigating patiently. Already he has enough material for an Encyclopædia Japonica. The thing he has to fight against is the influence of his surroundings, which tend to allay keen desire for achievement which scholars in the West maintain. In counteracting this, the septennial home-coming is a wholesome tonic.

On the west coast the nearest missionary to us was at Kanazawa. When we went there we fell by the wayside, as it were, returned to our former habits of life, sat on an American rocking-chair and slept on a spring bed. It was a sad fall from the floor up into a rocking-chair and on to a spring bed, but the missionary's hospitality was as difficult to resist as that of our native friends at Tatsumi.

One of our Hongwanji friends was with us on one of our journeys through Kanazawa. His home was in Kiyoto, where he had studied with interest the work of the teachers in Doshisha, the Christian college which American missionaries had established there over twenty years ago. He had been to America and to Europe; at Oxford had attracted some little attention by his industry in history and in philosophy. I believe he had been a student under Max Müller. He had a fine admiration for Christianity, and only asked for fair judgment.

"We are on good terms with the Doshisha folk," he said, as we went along on foot towards some famous hot springs a few ri south, "and we have learned much from them. Our priests have gone abroad to study religious institutions in the lands where this wonderful religion came from. Jesus seems to us much like what we call a Buddha. We notice, too, that Christianity is divided into sects much as Buddhism is. I think for the most part, though, that our sects get along together with less friction than do the Christian sects. At least we do not criticise each other in the newspapers. Perhaps at home you do not. I was only a student when I was abroad, and my text-books took so much of my time that I am sorry to say I did not read much else. I have seen rather unpleasant letters in the Yokohama and Kobe papers. I do not think the Doshisha folk contributed any of these letters.

"It seems unfair to me that we should be condemned without being studied. We do not wish to keep Christian missionaries out of Japan. We welcome them, for there is work enough to keep us all busy, but we should like to have those who come over to teach us the truth study our doctrines, to see if we have not already some of this truth ourselves. Here and there a missionary studies Buddhism, but the instances are not sufficient to make a large percentage of the men and women who come to live among us. How can they expect to teach the Japanese people if they do not understand the Japanese people? and how can they expect to understand the people unless they understand the people's religion? Why, our Foreign Office officials study Christianity before going abroad. That is part of their diplomatic training. How much more, then, should missionaries of religion study the faiths of the lands they go to?

"The good work that Christian missionaries are doing in Japan would progress more rapidly if the missionaries would learn the Buddhist doctrines and study the influence these doctrines have had on the minds of Japanese. Whatever there is of truth in the religion of Europe and America and in the religion of Japan must harmonise. I do not see why Buddhists and Christians should be at war. I do not believe they are at heart. We both should like to save the world, and we shall. To save the world, however, it is not necessary that one party should annihilate the other. It will be more in accordance with wisdom for each man to do whatever directly helpful work there is before him. There is so much to do, we cannot afford to expend even the minutest quantity of energy needlessly.

"Look at China, for instance, where we have some missionary interest. We may have some hard work there before long. We are foreigners there, you know, and the anti-foreign feeling is increasing. This is partly the fault of greedy European Powers and partly the fault of methods in missionary work. It

MISSIONARIES AND MISSIONARIES 223

is unfortunate that religion and statecraft should be mixed together, but to many Chinese to-day the foreign missionary is a sort of advance agent of the gunboat. Missionaries come and provinces go. The Chinese look upon this as cause and effect. Sequence in time is logical connection in their minds. You see they are a very old people, and are still living in the past. They know little of anything that is less than two thousand years old.

"Ieyasu, Mayor of the Palace, early in the seventeenth century thought the same of Spanish and Portuguese missionaries once, and ordered them to leave. Their refusal to do so led to a massacre. He was able to forestall foreign invasion because in his day Japan was far from the West, and the military abilities of the East and the West were more nearly on a footing. China is powerless to-day. She cannot defend herself.

"A convert is likely to get into trouble when he becomes a Christian, unless he is able to keep up a double set of subscriptions. To keep the peace he should pay sums regularly to his guilds and societies and to the mission he has joined. He is often too poor to do both, and if he gives his money to the mission his former friends and his relatives may annoy him. Suppose he is forced into a fight and is taken to jail, naturally he looks to the missionary. The missionary sees the German or French or English Consul, whichever it may be, who in his turn writes to the Minister Plenipotentiary at Peking, and the Minister goes to the " Tsung li Yamen," or Chinese Foreign Office. An official of the Tsung li Yamen then comes to the governor of the province in which the convert and the missionary live, and talks to His Excellency about the annoyance of foreign complications. The governor proceeds against the mayor or the chief of the town in which the convert is confined, and the mayor has it out with the convert's accusers. It reads like the story of *The House that Jack Built*, but it usually ends badly. The mayor is between the governor and the populace. He will have a hard time of it either way. The governor is afraid of the Tsung li Yamen, and will make trouble for him if he does not let the convert go. If he does liberate him the people will conspire against him for favouring an apostate. Not that the apostacy enrages them. They would forgive that would the convert continue his subscriptions. They need his money and are wroth with the missionary for depriving them of it.

"The missionary is also laying up trouble for himself by his lack of understanding of Chinese social institutions. For one thing, he should let the Chinese pay respect to their ancestors as much as they like. A Chinaman reverences his father and his mother, his grandfather, his grandmother, and all his ancestors. Living or dead his forefathers receive the same veneration. The Chinaman obeys your Fifth Commandment better than the Christian obeys it. He continues to pay his respects after death has taken his parents from him. He believes their spirits know of his fidelity, and that he is pleasing them by his acts of filial piety. He does not ask the spirits to assist him, or to protect him, or to do anything for

MISSIONARIES AND MISSIONARIES

him in any way. He does not pray to them nor does he worship them. He honours them.

"The missionary, not understanding what he saw, mistook the Chinese obeisance for an act of worship. This mistake has led him to protest against the most sacred of Chinese customs, and to irritate the people in their most sensitive spot. In fact, from the Chinese standpoint, the remarks of some of the Protestant missionaries as to the worthiness and the fate of 'heathen' ancestors, have been revolting. What would you say to the man who applied to your mother epithets that would shame a fallen woman? Kill him? Yes, that is your attitude, and it is the attitude of many Chinese towards the missionaries. You will see the result some day.

"We do not have this antagonism in Japan because the Japanese are tolerant and are eager to learn. We Buddhists are glad to work with all who will help mankind. Japanese reverence their ancestors, but they are not as keen about it as the Chinese are; and, altogether, Christian missionaries may be said to have a rather easy time of it here. If they will master our language and understand our doctrines they will have a yet easier time.

"And I should like to say, too, that some of those missionaries who are rather hot against Buddhism would see, if they would consider, that we are Buddhists for pretty much the same reason that accounts for their being Christians. Their parents were Christians, their relatives were, their friends were. They heard their learned men preach Christianity, their teachers told them it was true, and thus growing up in it they believe it. That is natural. If they did not, it would be remarkable. Buddhism came to us in the same way. We both did not know of other religions at first, and as each has the same practical end in view perhaps we can work better side by side than against each other. As there are many things about which a Christian missionary would find fault if he studied Buddhist sects, so there are points in some missionaries' teachings that we do not see clearly or do not think of great value to the world.

"We believe that good done for the sake of reward has no merit and will not benefit the individual who acts with such a motive. The Christians' heaven, as some preach it, seems to us a bribe. We do not claim to be the only folks that possess the truth. I have heard that this religion (Christianity) was the only true one, that others were all wrong—as filthy rags, I think the missionary said. Then he added that, of the forty or fifty kinds of Christianity, his kind was the only right kind. (I believe he was a member of what he called the Christian Church, and his followers were Christian Christians, instead of Baptist, or Methodist, or Presbyterian, or Episcopalian, or Unitarian Christians.) He said that if there could be such a thing as grades of joy in heaven, the Christian Christians would have the best grade.

"The Christian Bible, in which we find much that is noble and beautiful and sacred, seems to us to be two Bibles, one Jewish and one Gentile. The New Testament contains the fulfilment of the prophecies of the old, some say, but the Jews, the 'chosen people of God,' do not agree to this statement. As the Old

FIGHTING PRIESTS

Testament belongs to them, their opinion as to its meaning should have weight. Why do Christian priests preach from the Old Testament if the doctrine of immortality is not to be found there? What would Christianity be without immortality?

"We do not understand why it is that what Jesus taught and what Christians do are so different. Jesus said 'Love your enemies,' yet Christians are at war in some place or other almost all the time. How many Christians have Christians killed? And why? We do not find the answer in the teachings of Jesus.

"The Jews, too, seem to have been at war a great deal. A 'heathen' might suppose that there was something in Bible study which made a man desire to fight. Some of our Buddhists are very careful to live up to the idea 'thou shalt not kill.' They have their wooden clogs made with one support underneath instead of two so that they will step on fewer insects when walking. Though there have been many fighting priests who served their emperor loyally or defended their homes against assault, there have been no Buddhist wars at all.

"We do not understand how the doctrines of 'Eternal Punishment' and 'Remission of Sins' agree. We have heard so often of incarnations—they are ubiquitous and perennial—that the Christian story does not have much force. We believe in liberation rather than in sacrifice, and the story of Jehovah offering His Son seems to us to be a myth founded on ideas of human sacrifice similar to those the Druids held. New Japan is scientific and critical. She is learning to compare foreign ideas and to discriminate between them. At first she accepted them *in toto*, as there was no help for it. Her experience gave her nothing to gauge by. Such religious theories or schemes or plans, as the Fall of Man and his Redemption, will hardly meet with general acceptance, but I should think that Christianity could proceed without them."

CHAPTER XXVIII

GILDED WITH OLD GOLD

WE found the pace of the gilded youth in Japan quite as rapid as it is in other countries. In fact it was so fast that, as Walter Besant once said of a man who was running away from a bear, "it was manifest to the most casual observer that the primary effort was speed."

The Prince of Sendai set such a pace in the days of the Shogunate that the Mayor of the Palace remonstrated, and told him if he had money to get rid of he had better rid himself of it in a way that would be of some advantage to the State. Thereupon he ordered the Prince to dig a moat through Surugadai, the highest hill in Yedo. This moat completed a sort of spiral canal around the Shogun's palace. It took three thousand men two years to dig this ditch, which is known as "Sendai's Sorrow."

Sendai's chief exploit, one that brought him national notoriety, was hiring the entire Yoshiwara and closing the gates while he entertained his friends. The Yoshiwara is a community by itself on the outskirts of the city, and contains some one thousand nine hundred geisha and other persons whose lives, so long as they remain there, are dedicated to joy and sin. To hire the Carlton Hotel in order to eat a sandwich would be on a par, financially, with this act of Sendai's.

Sendai liked the "No" dance, which is indeed perfect in its dainty grace, but, like classic music, one cannot learn to appreciate it in an afternoon. A long course of training is necessary. This training is expensive when one persists in it on the scale that Sendai followed. He delighted to look over his saké cup while five hundred beautifully robed geisha postured before him in rhythmic motion, like a field of flowers in the wind. He gave great dances on all the festal days, sometimes on a flotilla in the river, and sometimes beneath the cherry blossoms along the banks of Sumida Gawa. He would hire a theatre, with a company of actors, and give a continuous performance for a week, with the little square pens in the pit filled with singing girls, all banqueting.

The tea-houses that he patronised grew rich, for his custom was to order "the best in the world and all there is of it." He would have broken the Satsuma dishes off which he fed if he had not been too thoroughly an artist.

He ate kami-boku, made of the little kernel of flesh taken from the head of "tai," a kind of bream much esteemed by Japanese epicures. Court nobles would have relished the bodies, but Sendai threw these away. He ate mountain-sparrow soup, that even the Shogun saw only once a year when he offered food to the spirits of his ancestors.

With all this he seems to have kept his health, owing, perhaps, to his practice of fencing with the

HERE HIDEYOSHI, THE TAIKO, DRANK HIS TEA

long two-handed bamboo swords that are popular to this day. The exercise is rougher than either broadsword or rapier, for which reason the fencers need well-padded armour. No European has a chance at sword-play against a Japanese expert, and with this two-handed weapon of the Prince of Sendai it was said that he could draw his sword and take off an enemy's head in a single sweep.

Of course, being a great swell, he had blades that were worth many times their weight in gold. One could not be a swell in those days without owning good swords, for "the sword was the soul of the samurai." Sendai, like others in his class, went in for archery too, and could shoot while standing in his stirrups or from under his horse's neck. Archery is still a gentleman's pastime in Japan; likewise polo, with scoop nets instead of mallets. It is rough work, but not as fierce as the game they play in India.

Tea-drinking hardly would seem to come under the head of a sport, or to appeal to a man who led a fast fierce life. But Sendai spent enough at it to make a dozen experts in its ceremonies independent for life. Of this pastime Professor Chamberlain says: "The art of drinking tea has gone through three stages —medico-religious, luxurious, and æsthetic." It was the third stage that appealed to Sendai.

The ceremony originated in a worthy cause. A priest named Eisai, who wished to reform a youthful Shogun who drank too much saké and sham-shiu, got him interested in tea by elaborating a diverting set of rules for drinking it. When the ceremony was well established in the august favour the old priest gave the Shogun tracts on the beneficial effects of tea, how it regulated the whole system and drove out devils—might, indeed, be preferred to the gold cure.

Eisai worked in a good deal of religion along with his tea, but the ceremony of drinking grew more and more worldly, until it was all luxury and no religion. The swells drank tea daily in gorgeous apartments hung with brocade and damask, where they burned precious perfumes, and served rare fishes and strange birds with sweetmeats and wine. In time they lost their fortunes and themselves in this extravagance of etiquette, for the rules ordained that all the things rich and rare that were exhibited were to be given to the singing and dancing girls who entertained the guests. Troops of them were always present, and this explains why Sendai was so fond of tea.

Even in such extravagant observance, however, tea-drinking was not altogether an evil. While it lasted it gave great stimulus to art. Some of the finest specimens of native work date from the "tea period."

CHAPTER XXIX

AND SO HE BECAME A SAINT

NACHI has waterfalls, temples, and big trees. The big trees are glorious in the autumn, the temples have many famous relics, and the waterfalls, among them the highest in Japan, will wash away all sin. When Gardner and I were down there we tried one, with gratifying results. We may return to it some day, should it seem advisable. It does one good to take a fall now and again.

The pool we chose for our ablutions was below "Ichi-no-taki," or No. 1 Fall, the largest of the three, which tumbles down a good three hundred feet. It was the very place that Saint Mongaku Shonin had soaked in continuously for three weeks some centuries before. A peasant woman showed us where he sat, and then sold us several pictures taken on the spot—ages after the event.

Mongaku portraits are common in Nachi. They are accurate representations of what was in the mind of whoever made them. No one should blame the saint that they are not beautiful. He has quite enough else to answer for, and were it not for the virtues of Ichi-no-taki, and his long atonement in the pool below, one dreads to think where he would be now. Mongaku was the name he was known by after death; his living name was Rambo. Rambo's experience was one to have made of him a saint or else a raging devil. Fate ordained him saint, with a purgatory on earth.

When young he had been full of fiery ambitions. His father was dead, and being the only son what could his mother do? Her parents had "augustly departed," and her husband too; was not her's the third obedience? Rambo was not much about the house, however, nor keen for the books that his uncle, the chief priest at Fudarakuji, the first of the Kwannon temples, gave him to read. He was for the mountains. He knew the Kumano Three Peaks better than the oldest hunters, at least so said the village folk. He was a wonderful swimmer too, and could dive into pools and catch fishes with his hands. Occasionally he would be away for weeks at Oshima, watching with the whalers and going out with them to place the nets. He was the first to jump on the dying mammal to cut the slits in the creature's back and make the hawser fast for towing the body ashore. Both on land and on the water, and in the water too, he was as skilful at eighteen as others were at eight-and-thirty. Furthermore, he was a handsome youth, according to traditions, not the pictures, and had small traces about him of the saint that was to be.

One day of a season that had been poor for whales, Rambo had been with the topmost look-outs watching vainly for a chance to give the signal to the men

AND SO HE BECAME A SAINT

below, when a messenger from his mother came to him with tidings that Shinrui San of Kanazawa, his kinsman by adoption, would be in Nachi soon. His mother wished to have everything in readiness for the guest from such a distance, and begged Rambo so to order it. Rambo had never seen this kinsman, but he had heard of him as a man of prowess, one after his own heart, so he returned quickly with the messenger and prepared to receive Shinrui.

The guests were two days late in reaching Nachi, owing to the fall of an embankment, which came down upon the road, making it impassable for half a ri. Shinrui could have come round by a footpath probably, but Gozen his wife was with him, and to climb the mountain with her would be more troublesome than to wait for men to clear the road. Mongaku chafed at the delay, and threatened to go back to Oshima, but his mother persuaded him to stay, saying that now that her brother-in-law, Gozen's father, was dead, and the mother also, and the young couple were coming to them, everything possible should be ready to give them a welcome to Nachi, as if it were their own home, as indeed, with her son's permission, she hoped it might be.

"It is of no matter to me," said Rambo. "I wish to see Shinrui, for he is a brave samurai and famous as a hunter. I can exercise with him. If he will stay I shall be glad. I can show him the whales, too, if ever they come to this coast again. He has no such sport off Kanazawa. If my cousin stays too, it will do perhaps. I can tell when I see her. But she must be a daughter to you and company, if you need such things."

These words pleased the mother greatly, for the days had been long and lonely since she became a widow.

"Your selfish, stupid mother thanks you with much gratefulness," she said, bowing to her son, who was busy making a net for ducks and did not notice.

On the following day after this talk, Shinrui came and O Gozen San with him. Rambo's mother greeted them with many welcomes.

"It is indeed good to see you," she said. "Come in! come in! My son has gone to the river for some trout and will be back directly. What a pity there should have been an accident to the embankment! We heard of it only yesterday, but it explained your delay. Indeed we hardly thought you could arrive before night, or possibly to-morrow morning. Here! I will put your luggage in this cupboard where you can open it at your leisure. This corner of our unworthy house is to be yours always. Excuse the dirty and miserable condition of everything. Do you like the view across the river to the hillside temple? The bath will be hot in a few minutes. Here are the futon. Lie down and rest, and I will call you presently. Here is some hot saké. Pardon the rude way in which I serve it. Now I will leave you and send a messenger for Rambo."

So in a short time the new arrivals had bathed and rested and refreshed themselves with cakes and saké, and by the time for the midday meal Rambo was

AND SO HE BECAME A SAINT 237

back with a basket of fish such as gives joy to the hearts of the children of Japan. Shinrui and O Gozen San bowed low and apologised for their slow coming, and for the trouble they were giving, and for having the "disgusting effrontery to be in existence," as well as for other things beyond the ken of those uninitiated to the mysteries of Japanese etiquette. Rambo bowed with due formality, and then, not noticing O Gozen San, who, after the manner of Japanese women, kept herself on the verge of obliteration, he proceeded to ask about the sports of the west coast,—the fencing, the wrestling, the boar hunting, the bear and the deer, the ducks and the pheasants, about the dangers of the mountains, the storms on the North Sea, and what not.

In the afternoon he took Shinrui to show him the falls and the pools where the fishing was best. The next day the pair went into the mountains, and later they travelled down to see if the whales had come in sight. One did come in towards shore, and the Oshima men got him. Shinrui was astonished at what he saw. Soon after they were home again Shinrui had to go to Kiyoto on business connected with the estate of the man who had adopted him. It was then that Rambo really saw O Gozen San. The shyness which her new surroundings caused at first had disappeared, and her new mother, as she called her hostess, had treated her so kindly that the cheerfulness she had not known since her father's death returned.

Rambo watched her often, though he did not realise why. He had not thought seriously of any woman before, nor cared much whether or no there were such beings; but now, his mother noticed, he was round the house much more, sometimes the whole day long; he was more careful of his dress, and of his appearance generally; when he was away it was only to procure some dainty, which, though he did not present it directly to O Gozen San, he encouraged her to eat with much solicitude.

The old lady did not suspect the meaning of the change, until she said one morning—

"Shinrui San will return soon, now. You will then have a companion for your hunting. I see how you have missed him. It is too bad you should have had a stupid time so long about the house where only women are."

"I do not wish Shinrui to return," said Rambo. There will be no peace for me when he comes back. I wish the gods would take him to the Bonin islands."

"Oya! oya!" cried the old lady, "what can cause you to talk so of a friend, and our relation?"

"That is just the matter. He is a relation. If he were not, all would be easy. But I must have my way in spite of that. You must arrange it for me."

"Arrange what, my son?"

"I must have O Gozen San. She must go with me and be my wife."

"Are you mad? Why do you make such horrid jests? Surely you do not mean these words. You would not harm the honour of our house?"

But Rambo convinced his mother, whose face

AND SO HE BECAME A SAINT

was hidden in her sleeves, that he was in earnest, and was determined to have his way despite all obstacles. She had always done his bidding, she must do so now.

"No, no, you may kill me but I cannot," was the hapless woman's reply. Rambo was in such a rage that no one knows what he might have done, had not O Gozen San, who had been in the next room and had heard all through the karakami that shut off her apartment, rushed out, and clutching her new mother's sleeve, turned to her cousin and said slowly and distinctly—

"Do not urge your mother now, or vex her with reproaches. There is no reason to do so. I am willing to do as you wish, on one condition which I will explain to you apart." Then stepping to the farther end of the room she talked with Rambo in a low voice, lest the mother hear.

"It would never do to run away together and leave my husband to follow us. We might both lose our lives. You must await his return, and at night when he is asleep put an end to him. We can then live in peace without fear of molestation."

There was fierce joy in Rambo's heart on hearing O Gozen San speak these words. To kill Shinrui would be a simple matter, and he readily agreed to await his home-coming. Turning to his mother, he said—

"All is settled; have no more fear."

He had not long to wait. Gozen's husband returned three days later, and that night Rambo feasted him and saw that his saké cup was never empty. When Shinrui was beginning to show the effects of this attention, Rambo, saying he would return shortly, left the room to put his sword in order. O Gozen San sat by her husband, helping in the plot, and pouring him saké until he yawned and called for his futon. She got some and laid them out in order.

Not noticing what they were, nor in what place she had arranged them, he rolled over to them and immediately was asleep. Then wistfully Gozen looked at him, and drawing the yagu up to cover him, she bowed her head to the floor, saying—

"Dana San, O Yasumi Nasai."

Closing the karakami to her apartment she changed the dark kimono she was wearing for one all white. Then she laid out Shinrui's own futon in the accustomed place, took a rosary that once had been her mother's, and kneeling with the beads between her palms, she repeated slowly several times—

"Namu Amida Butsu! Namu Amida Butsu!"

And now lying down she covered herself with Shinrui's yagu, and lay as though asleep quite in the position her husband had been wont to occupy. Only she herself knew it was the woman and not the man that lay there.

What happened afterwards who shall say? But in the morning a moaning mother's mind had given way through grief for a son's crime; a husband had been drowned in searching fiercely for a murderer; and a youth of splendid promise had turned from the world with the horror of remorse upon him, with a great awakening in his soul, a cry demanding life-long penance and self-obliterating service to the glory of Amida Buddha. The service he began in the sanctuary pool of penitents, which to this day is beneath the great fall at Nachi.

CHAPTER XXX

KADE AND THE REPEATERS

WE had a pupil in one of our classes for English conversation whom we called "Pokan no Kade"—or "Kade," for short. When Pokan no Kade was a youngster his particular playmate was Mutsu Hito, the present Emperor of Japan.

Mutsu and Kade had many likes in common, and many dislikes too; but they were generous lads, and had never been known to quarrel. Difference in rank had not come between them, and each one was devoted to the other, as two chums should be. One of their common likes was cakes. There was much discussion about the palace whether Kade or the Son of the Immortals ate this sweet of the pastry-maker with the more relish. Certainly it was a joyous sight to see either of them a-munching, and when they munched together, as they often did in the palace garden, even the fiercest of the guardsmen would begin to purr.

But one day there was no cake. The Son of the Immortals had had a pain that morning, and the thirteen Court physcians, after consultation, had told the Grand Marshal of the Household about this pain. The grand marshal told the chamberlain, who told the keeper of the royal purse, who told the imperial provider, who told the high caterer, who told the dispenser of the sacred pastry, that cake was the cause of the ache. Eleven minutes later there was no cake to be found in the royal palace.

When Mutsu said "cake" to the noble to whose charge he had been committed for the day, that functionary bowed low, and told the officer next in rank that the Son of the Immortals wished for cake. This officer, in turn, bowed to the ground and then repeated the royal wish to an officer still lower, and so it went on; but cake did not appear.

"Chin no Kwashi doko ka?" cried Mutsu—which being interpreted means, "Where is my cake?" The noble guardian bowed low, and said to the officer below him, "The Son of the Immortal Ones has deigned to say, 'Where is my cake?'" These words were also repeated, and many others, petulant, wrathful, and beseeching; but that which was longed for did not come.

The palace and the grounds about echoed with the voices of officers and servants of many grades, who were as the links of a chain, beginning at the feet of the Son of the Immortals and ending nowhere—at least, not in the cake pantry. The air was full of the word "cake," but the *thing* cake came not in sight.

While all this was going on, Pokan no Kade sat on a pile of sand near the great man of the palace, playing with a half-dozen watches which his Imperial chum had given to him the day before. Watches, or "toki," as Mutsu had called them, were new things in Japan then, especially repeaters, and all six of these were repeaters.

Kade had great fun with them, ringing their bells, and laying them like stepping-stones about a dainty garden such as all Japanese children can lay out in miniature so prettily. Once he built a castle, and planted the watches in two piles on the very top, just as the gold dolphins are put on the Castle of Nagoya.

He was so busy with his play that for a long time he did not hear the many voices saying "cake." But finally, when an inadvertent kick had upset his castle, and he was looking about for something else to do, he heard the cries, and soon found out their meaning.

Thrusting the watches into his sleeve—which was large enough to hold more playthings than the pockets of a whole suit of clothes such as an English boy wears—he ran to the royal kitchen; but of course there was no cake there, nor would the cooks make any, though Kade begged never so hard.

"I'll get some, anyhow," he said to himself. "A watch is as pretty as a cake. I know where there's an old woman with a houseful of cakes. She just sits and looks at them all day. I'll go to see her."

So Kade slipped out unseen and went to the cake-shop, where he laid the six watches on the floor near where the old woman sat, and picking up six of the prettiest cakes, put them in his sleeves, and scampered back to the palace.

That night the Court physicians held another consultation.

CHAPTER XXXI

KADE WOULD ADVENTURE

KADE thought to run away from his home one night. He had planned for the adventure as he sat on the edge of the verandah of his home in Tokio. Years after he told us the story. Here it is in substance, if not in his exact words.

"Yes, I must have waraji, of course," he said to himself as he sat swinging his bare legs to and fro. "The road over the mountain is rough. I remember how it cut my feet when I got out of the kago up there and ran on ahead to see if the men had caught a bear. If I had only worn sandals then I could have gone into the woods and helped."

Kade was only nine years old then, and though of a Kuge or Court noble family had been adopted by a personage who stood high in favour with the Shogun. He knew the folk-lore of his country well, and believed it all was true, and he could tell of many of the brave deeds that had been done in Dai Nippon since Jimmu Tenno, the founder of the Empire, had descended from the skies upon the sacred mountain that all Japanese still hold in reverence. His tutor had told him of these things, for he was a man of war as well

KADE WOULD ADVENTURE

as learning, and he found a ready listener in the lad whom the daimiyo had given into his charge.

Kade wished to do great things, too. He had just made up his mind to go over the mountains to a place where lived the most valiant of all the clans, the great clan of Satsuma. There he would learn the art of war by actual fighting, and would win fame for himself and honour for his house.

He was to start out that very night, and it was time to make ready. All that he knew was that his goal was over the mountains, that the road was rough, that he needed waraji and that waraji cost money. He did not know what money was, for, like other children of gentle birth in Old Japan, he had never bought anything in his life, nor even touched a coin or a piece of script; but he had heard the steward of the household talking about money one day while counting bright pieces of something yellow, and he knew where those bright pieces were kept.

"I am almost sure they were money," he said, as he went on with his planning to run away from home to be a soldier.

"I'll get some of them as soon as everyone is in bed to-night, and then everything will be all right. I'll go down to the shop by the stone bridge and give the money to the old woman in the sandal shop, and she will give me the waraji."

So when all was still throughout the house Kade crawled out from the futon where he had been lying as though fast asleep, and sliding back the karakami and the shoji, and the little door to the outside, made his way quickly to the hut near Ishibashi, as the old stone bridge is called. He had with him the wooden box in which he had seen the steward put the shining yellow pieces.

The sandal maker was a light sleeper, and heard the first low call that Kade made. She found the kind of waraji that he wanted, and he thanked her for them. Then he opened the wooden box and handed her a piece of money.

When the sandal maker saw it she gasped for breath. Kade had offered her a gold piece stamped jiu yen. A jiu yen piece! Why, that was enough to buy six thousand waraji, or sixty thousand likely. It was more money than the old woman had seen in all her life. She had heard of such enormous pieces, but that she should ever touch one with her poor old hand—

"Come, take it," said Kade. "It's money. I must put on the waraji and be off."

The old woman was still speechless.

The lad called out to her again, but there was no answer. Then the moon broke through a cloud and shone upon the aged face. When Kade saw it, fear came upon him, and he ran back to his uncle's house so fast that he seemed to fly. He took with him the wooden box and the waraji, but he left the jiu yen piece in the dead woman's hand, where a guardsman found it in the early morning.

CHAPTER XXXII

WHAT HAPPENED TO ALLEN

SHE is so frolicsome, jolly, and good-natured, and above all she delights so much in pleasing, that globe-trotters, the "transients" of Japan, misunderstand the "musume," while she is too innocent to understand their views of her. They think she cannot say "no," but she can. They think, too, that complacency is the law of her life. There they are right and wrong, for she accepts what her conscience tells her is her duty with a resignation that has the outward aspect of complacency, but she is far indeed from being complacent with infringements of those proprieties that are natural to the social conditions of her far-distant land.

She can draw the line for the globe-trotter, and for the foreigner resident, too, for that matter, as one of our friends knows full well, or did know until a log rolled over him in a Western lumber camp and blotted out all memory of the past, so that even tapping his sub-consciousness has not recalled it.

He was an American with various degrees which he had picked up here and there, and a keen fondness for travel. He was M.A. of Harvard, LL.B.

of Columbia, Ph.D. of Heidelberg, J.V.D. of Paris; and something else in St. Petersburg that is impossible in English type. While he had been picking up degrees he had done what he called "a few stunts on the side," running a paper in one place, and lecturing on philosophy, Sanscrit, Greek, French literature, and the History of Law in other places. In truth he had an appalling quantity of education, and in spite of it much charm of manner. He came to Japan as a sociologist. He wished to study whatever relics of the recent feudalism might remain, and to watch the progress in the national kindergarten.

With his string of degrees he had no trouble in finding a university appointment that gave him the opportunities he needed for investigation. A Dai Gakko professor ranks high in Japan. Soon he was established. He rented a home on Small Stone-River Hill, near a famous temple, and had arranged his life quite on the Japanese order. Excepting when he was in the lecture-room he wore "kimono" instead of foreign dress, and "geta," or clogs, instead of shoes. He went barefoot, ate with chopsticks, sat on the floor, slept on the floor, learned to like raw fish and plain boiled rice. He had not a stove in the house, only the charcoal braziers, called hibachi, and a sort of furnace for burning wood that the cook used in the kitchen. The smoke from this found its way out through a hole high up in the wall under one end of the ridge pole at the top of the ceilingless kitchen, or else it blew round and pervaded the apartment generally. The gas from the charcoal got out easily too, for the ventilation in Japanese houses is particularly thorough.

Allen, whom, by the way, the natives called Sensei (first-born), a title of respect to scholars, professional men, and old gentlemen generally, went so far as to master the Japanese pillow. This was a triumph, the fame of it spread abroad. The newspapers got hold of it, and made diagrams of the process of the achievement, picturing Allen in all manner of contorted shapes as the result of "first attempts." In the serenity of his ultimate attainment he dreamed such dreams as only a Japanese artist can depict or a Japanese paper would dare to print.

When he had made himself familiar with his new environment, a kind of thing he had especial aptitude for, he fell in love. That was natural enough and proper. He could not well have helped it even had it not been proper, as any other man would say had he known O Toku San. She was one of a class of girls that came to Allen's house for an hour's English conversation exercise each afternoon. At first he was in love with the whole dozen of them, but gradually, though he did not love eleven less, he loved O Toku San more. She had clear brown eyes, that glowed and flashed and sparkled merrily, and changed as one looked at them, showing wonder at Allen's words, then comprehension, and then delight at the possession of new knowledge. It is not strange that the instruction wandered now and then, deviating from the "system" the instructor had laid down on psychologic principles for harmonious development according to the laws of thought.

All the twelve learned rapidly, as is the custom of girls in Dai Nippon, but O Toku got hopelessly ahead, so far, indeed, that Allen's system wore itself to ravels catching up — and then it never reached her. He put her into French to hold her back, and later into German; and finally he gave her a series of essays on general literature that he had worked up for a P.G. course for some college down in Melbourne. In this composition he had used whatever language had come handiest. For French he had used German, for German French, and for English both French and German. O Toku San was equally indifferent in her reading of the essays, and one day, bowing very low, she handed to Allen the whole series written out in Japanese, saying she thought all students would like to read it if they could have it in their language. Allen had the translation printed, with O Toku's name and family crest on the title-page—the last page in the book as European volumes go — and six months later the Empress sent the girl a special decoration.

While all this acquisition was in progress, Allen was growing very chummy round at O Toku San's home, just off the corner of the famous Denzuin temple grounds. This home had been a temple in itself once, and all the paraphernalia of Buddhist worship was still in place in the chief apartment of the building; but with the disappearance of the Shogun and the reappearance of the Mikado, the Government had disestablished Buddhism, and the

WHAT HAPPENED TO ALLEN

priests had abandoned many temples for lack of the funds needful to maintain them. O Toku San's home was one of these abandoned temples. The beautiful shaft of light-brown stone standing by the gateway declared that eaters of flesh and drinkers of wine must not enter within the sacred precincts; but the fair maid's father troubled little about this ancient warning, and gave banquets almost every seventh day with beef and saké much in evidence.

Allen was much in evidence too on these occasions, and most of his spare moments between times also, so that his brethren at the University took it upon themselves to warn him against the danger of over-study in the electric climate of Japan. They suspected the new-comer of trying to break the record made by a young German professor who had learned to read, write, and speak Japanese within twelve months, and had never been right since. Allen thanked them, and said he would knock off at the first moment he felt unwell. Then he hired an extra man for his jin-riki-sha and pushed for Little Stone-River Hill as fast as he could go. Getting into his kimono, he "ran over" to pass the time until the twelve should assemble for their conversation lesson.

It was delicious lying on the porch there on the soft mats just within, listening to O Toku San as she read some favourite bit of foreign literature he had brought to her, and answering the questions she asked of the customs of the lands on the other side of the world. And what a tremendous thing a little question was sometimes—or its answer, rather!

He had lived in many countries and had studied much, but time and again O Toku San had him. His inheritance and hers had been so different. She would ask about some chance allusion in the text—a question that would never occur to a youth in Europe or America, for it referred to what was of the life there, which everyone in those countries knew unconsciously, and Allen would realise there was more in heredity, evolution, and development than he had ever dreamed of.

He had made much progress in Japanese, but that did not aid him. Had he known the sum total of languages in the Far East, his vocabulary would have been lacking. Intellectually, she was a child of China, he of Greece and Rome and the ancient Hebrews. If their family trees had any roots in common, it must have been in the days when their ancestors lived among the branches with foliage for clothes. He would go through the history of the half of the world he knew about, and she would listen, but it was all so different to the other half whose 800,000,000 people and their history he, like others, treated almost flippantly, that she could scarcely comprehend, she said so sadly.

"You should go abroad. Then you would soon understand," said Allen, "for you would see with your own eyes."

"I wish it very much, but I am only the little Japanese girl," replied O Toku San.

"And why can't the little Japanese girl go?" asked Allen. "The foreigners won't eat you."

"No, I know they are all kind, but next year my parents make me a marriage and I have not time for travels. Japanese women must be at home."

She spoke gently, with a low, sweet voice, as do all women in Japan. There was not a trace of bitterness in the tones, nor any intimation of complaining. That her longing should be considered or even noticed never crossed her mind. In her day the musume never had such thoughts.

Allen thought of none of these things just then, however. The word "marriage" had hit him hard. Another realisation was upon him, and O Toku San was again the cause.

"No, you must not marry," he said. "You are too young. You must go to Europe and to America to study; and besides I love you, and I want you to be *my* wife."

The man of many degrees had spoken words he would have laughed to scorn an hour earlier; and as for O Toku San, her heart stopped beating nearly. She looked at Allen with such a look as only perfect faith can give, and said slowly—

"I am very glad and have greatest astonishment you care for such foolish girl as I am all the time. I love you by all my heart because—because— it is very wonderful and how I cannot translate why, but you are kind and my most best good friend."

That was a long speech for a Japanese girl to make, and probably none ever made one so long before. Allen had taken her hand and was saying many things, when O Toku San's mother entered, saying—

"O Sanji go fun mai degozaimasa" ("Honourable Three five minutes before augustly-existing is"). And with that Allen made off for his conversation, and O Toku, whom custom forbade walking in the streets with a man other than her father, clattered along two minutes later.

The lesson was mostly with the eleven other girls that afternoon, for Allen said hardly a word to O Toku San, nor did she ask questions. To his disgust the August Sensei had to show himself at an official ball at the Rokumeikwan that evening, so he did not see O Toku San again until the next midday, when to his chagrin her mother sat out the entire visit. This annoyed him seriously, but it seemed the old lady had a purpose in her presence. She had been glad at first at the kind attentions of the foreigner who taught her daughter with so much care, but now she was worried. Falling in love was a thing she knew nothing about from personal experience, but she had heard of such indiscretions, and wished to protect O Toku from any such misfortune. The girl must marry soon. She had been engaged since before she was born, for her father had promised his first daughter to a chum's first son long ago when he was a student in "The Bureau for the Investigation of Barbarian Literature," now grown into the Imperial University. Neither of the young men had married then, but they engaged their prospective children nevertheless, and the engagement held. That it could be otherwise was one of those ideas that "is not" in the Japanese mind, for Japanese society has developed on Eastern not on Western lines,—and O Toku San's mother wished to avoid entanglements that might make the inevitable unpleasant.

She was always about when Allen went round to coach O Toku San in the foreign language lessons, and she told the girl she must not talk so much in English, but should use the native Japanese instead. She forgot that language as an instrument for the interchange of thought might be written as well as spoken, and so said not a word against notes and letters. And so a small miracle came about. Allen, for once in his life, became a correspondent of decent regularity. Written messages passed each way each day between O Toku and himself. The girl longed to become Allen's wife, and was doing all in her power to escape the engagement of such long standing.

"I am often kiss your photograph," she declared, "and wondering, 'Oh, where is my lover?' all the time you are not by me."

This was sweet to Allen, but to be so near O Toku San and yet have her always out of reach was tantalising. It began to tell on him. He saw he must have a change of scene or break down altogether. He told his friends at the University that he was going to the interior to investigate the subject of land tenure in several of the provinces. He would have carried O Toku San with him had she been willing to elope. She would not go, but at the moment of his leave-taking, when her mother had slipped into the next room for an instant to get a fresh cup of tea, she said to him—

"When you are in the country, please have a housekeeper to look after you, and I will look upon her as my sister."

She was in bed three days with what the doctors called "Shinkei-byo" (nerve-sickness) after he had gone. Prescriptions did no good; but the postman who called when the mother happened to be at the market worked a cure that anyone but a Christian Scientist would have marvelled at. Perhaps he was a Buddhist Scientist. Regular correspondence between the lovers, however, was hard to manage, owing to maternal vigilance, and in a few months Allen was back again to see if progress had been made in the destruction of that engagement.

He found that O Toku San had not yet seen the man she was engaged to, but that, so far as she had ventured to ascertain, her father's intention as to the marriage had not altered, and her mother's mind of course was "inside" her father's.

More land-tenure then, thought Allen, and was about leaving for the interior a second time, when a cable called him to America. Someone was dead, and there were affairs in the north-west that demanded his immediate attention. He had just time to catch his steamer, but he sent a note of love and explanation to O Toku San by a friend, and wrote to her soon after his arrival in Seattle, telling her of certain moneys he had come into, and asking her to wait patiently a little when he would be able to return to Japan to get her—his own little girl for ever.

Six weeks later came this reply—

"Sir,—I am married, and is called Mrs. Sodesuka. And by our Japanese morality and my natural temperament I decline for ever your impliteness letter,   Sodesuka O Toku."

CHAPTER XXXIII

THE SPORTSMAN IN JAPAN

WE were sitting round the charcoal fire glowing in a huge hibachi at the Jobugwaisha one crisp autumn morning, drinking "tea" made from roasted wheat, and waiting for the betto to bring our horses out. A jolly place it was in those days, but the Hachioji railway station has obliterated all trace of it.

As we prodded the coals and sipped the tea we discussed plans for the morrow. Suddenly Count Kuro, our champion rider, and own cousin of Pokan no Kade, went out on the "engawa," the narrow verandah that ran along the edge of the lounging rooms of the Riding Association, and pointed towards the east. "Ducks!" he shouted, "now I know what we can do to-morrow."

"What may that be?" asked a lean, bright-eyed man in a suit of foreign clothes that had done duty in an American university years before, and now pretty well disguised the fact that he was a Minister of State. He watched the couple of broad V's in the distance sailing south towards Kobe, as Kuro waved towards them, and said, "Those are ducks without doubt, but we cannot get at them."

"Oh! they are quite safe as far as any one of us is concerned," said Kuro; "but there is no reason why we should not have some others if you like. To-morrow will be Nichiyobi, and after we have done riding in the rings here why not stay on our horses until we reach my miserable hovel in the country. It's only a little farther than Oji, as you may do me the honour to remember. We can make it in time for lunch, and then try the nets so long as the light holds."

Not one of us said "no"; so the next morning, after we had done our prettiest work with the extra manœuvres that Nichiyobi always brought, we took to the road through Ueno and Komagome to Oji, and in less than two hours reached the "miserable hovel." I wish all our homes were as miserable. It is not overstating the case to say that the misery we saw there and underwent personally we were able to endure without a murmur. It was one of the places Kuro's father, the Governor of Tokio, had handed over to his son on retiring from office and becoming inkiyo. The house was low, and rambled along three sides of a parallelogram. It stood near the centre of a piece of land that measured some fifty thousands of tsubo. There were miniature lakes well stocked with fish, a stream in which in springtime one found trout, a house for the especial purpose of drinking tea, various gardens for flowers in the different seasons, a splendid collection of kiku, and away down in a corner, half a mile from the "hovel," the duck-pond.

Here we gathered after lunch. There must have

been a couple of hundred ducks in the pond, but there was quite room enough for them, and evidently they had not lacked for sustenance. If they had wished to seek for better board and lodgings elsewhere they could not do so, for the pond was in a cage.

Two of Kuro's helpers entered this cage as we arrived, and stepped into small punts. Then they poled along the edge of the pond and raised several gates, which opened into canals leading out from the cage in various directions. Kuro gave each of us a net on the end of a pole, much like a fisherman's landing-net, and stationed us at points on opposite sides of the canals. When we were in position he called out "Yoroshiii!" and a great quacking and fluttering began. The men in the punts drove the ducks as best they might up to the gates and through into the canals. It was not an easy job for the drivers, for many of the birds were shy of the openings, but enough came through to keep us men busy with our nets.

Our trick was to land them either as they swam, or on the wing as they rose out of the canals. The ease and the difficulty of doing this depend much on the depth and the width of the canal, on the netter's skill, and on the ducks. There were seven of us, and we caught between forty and fifty before sundown. Some we put back in the cage again, and the others we in due course incorporated. Kuro had given his steward a word before we came down to the pond, with the result that when we reached the house with our bags the "hovel" looked more like the stage setting for an old Greek drama than like a gentleman's country residence. Another feast confronted us.

"Ippai o nomu nasai," said Kuro to me when the first dance was over, and he handed saké cups to Gardner and to me from a basin of water before him where they had been floating. We condescended and so did he. Then he said—

"That was rather easy work this afternoon, just enough to finish off a lunch with and make one ready for a bit of supper. I wish you two would come with me to my uncle's on the west coast, to see how they net ducks there. It is more interesting; and Fukui, near where he lives, is a famous town. It was in that country, in ancient times, that the Chinese and Korean embassies used to arrive. If you come, you will learn something of our history and our wild ducks too." Such a combination of easily-to-be-attained knowledge was irresistible. Off we went.

Kuro's uncle was a fine old samurai—a knight of the days gone by, who had fought for the restoration. He proved to us that hospitality was every whit as warm on the west coast as on the east. The day after our arrival he gave us a lesson in "Sakudori," as he called netting for ducks. Kuro knew all about it, but he paid as much attention to his uncle's discourse as if he had never heard of the art before. Then the old gentleman took us up over the hills near his home and showed us the positions that the hunters take when waiting for the ducks either in the evening or the early morning. Small posts, each with a number, marked these positions.

"You see the ducks come up this way in the morning and from the opposite direction in the evening. They always go over these hills. It has been their custom ever since the hills were here. Our plan for their capture is simply to intercept them. I will explain better to-night, when several of my friends will be here from the Duck Club that has leased these hills. Watching them, and trying as they try, will soon teach you all there is to know. You see these numbers on the posts. They correspond with numbers on little wooden tickets which the members have. A member has the same ticket for two mornings and two nights, then he changes with another member — and so on in rotation, so that no one member may have too many chances at a good stand or too many absences of chances at a poor stand."

About four o'clock that afternoon twenty of us set out, all in native dress, with straw sandals, straw rain-coats, straw leggings, and huge straw hats like umbrellas, that fitted to our heads with a bamboo framework and tied under our chins. When squatted on the ground we looked like small ricks of straw that not even a duck would suspect. Our weapons looked like fish-poles, but they were not. They were slender masts on which we hung nets, much as the square sails are rigged to the mast of a ship. We set out with our poles over our shoulders, like a band of spearmen in feudal times, and with a half-dozen attendants with stacks of lacquered boxes full of things the kitchen-folk had been preparing all the day.

"When you see the ducks," said Kuro, after we had

taken our places, "get your pole ready to toss up, and be sure you don't have the edge of the net turned towards the birds. Have it spread out wide, and throw it square in front of them. As soon as you can judge their speed and direction you'll be all right. There they come! Be ready."

We were all crouched low with our hands on our poles, and a minute later the air was full of nets and a tremendous clatter of quacks. Four nets had been successful, and had performed the act of interception to a nicety. One of the nets went far afield, however, it having met a duck that was a drake, and a right lusty one he was, for he gave the attendants a chase of over a mile. I learned how not to throw sideways, and once came very near landing a beauty. Gardner had actually caught a drake, while Kuro had three and uncle five, the largest number anyone had, but luck had favoured him with a "double," a very rare occurrence,—one bird following another directly into the net.

The next day Kuro said, "Suppose we go over to Noto and shoot some 'yama kujira.' There's good pheasant shooting too. The farmers would be grateful to you for killing kujira, for they do so much damage to the crops. It's a wheat country over there, you see, and the fields have fences all about to keep the kujira out. You'll seldom see a fence on farms anywhere else in Japan. We can put up at Hongwanji temples. I know some of the priests. In fact some of them are relations of mine, and you being a foreigner will be doubly welcome. Most of Noto has never seen a foreigner."

All the time he was talking, Gardner and I had been wondering what "yama kujira" could mean. "Kujira" meant whale and "yama" meant mountain. What could whales be doing in wheat-fields or on mountains? Impossible, of course. So I said—

"Kuro, my honourable friend, you have deigned to make the august joke."

"What! you don't know mountain whale?" he asked. "That is very famous wherever there is Buddhism in Japan. It is an old name, fifteen hundred years perhaps. The first Buddhist priests here tired of the same kind of fish and vegetables every day without any meat, and one of them discovered a way to escape from so much monotony. 'It is wrong to eat flesh,' he said, 'but to eat whale is lawful. We will call deer mountain whale and then we may eat venison as much as we like.' So he began, and many others followed his example."

Noto proved to be as interesting as Kuro had suggested. "Whales" were plentiful, and pheasants also, while the Hongwanji priests offered us more hospitality than it was possible to accept. Every temple we came to had a "matsuri" on the day of our arrival. We had never seen so many festivals consecutively. It was Kuro's doing, I fancy, though he would not own up to it. From Noto we went up into the mountains and tried for bear and wild boar. We had some luck with them and plenty of excitement. Some of the native hunters are extremely skilful with their spears. We met one who had run as high as sixty for his winter's work.

New Year saw us in Tokio, but we came back to

the west coast again for fishing and for monkeys. We knew the salmon fishing already. It is quite the same in Japan as it is in England, and the trout fishing too, though Kuro had a way of using small fish as decoys that was interesting.

"I'll coax them," he said one day when we had made several casts and got nothing. He took a hand-net and went to a bit of a stream that flowed into the one we were whipping. Presently he cried, "Now we're ready. See what these will do," and he showed me wiggly things the size of whitebait. "I'll just put a bit of black thread to each of them," he continued, "let them down the brook, and draw them up a few times and we shall have something large enough to eat." He was a prophet, for two hours later we had a mess that sufficed not only for ourselves but for the entire household of the temple in which we were staying.

The fishing we enjoyed most, however, was down Gifu way. "I'll show you an old Japanese custom for night-fishing which perhaps you cannot see in England," remarked Kuro as we journeyed south. "We have not packs of hounds for hunting like the English, because we cannot ride in paddy-fields, but we have packs of birds for fishing: cormorants you call them. It is an old custom, for our most ancient poetry speaks of it. The birds know the business well, as you will see. They have good training."

Indeed they had. We were out in a boat on the river the next night with a bonfire at one end of the craft and a screamy squawking lot of cormorants in the water about us, which two men kept hold of by means of reins of spruce fibre, guided them, yelling and splashing at them with sticks, disentangling them when they got too badly mixed up, and unloading them when their pouches were quite filled. Each bird had a ring round its neck which prevented it swallowing all but the smaller fishes, and a band round its body with a handle at the top with which to lift it in and out of the water. The men with the reins had their hands full, for they had sixteen hungry, excited birds to manage which dived and flopped in sixteen directions at once. The fire at the bow was the bait that brought the fish to the surface of the water in reach of the fatal beaks which gobbled them in at an astounding rate—the birds averaging over a hundred fishes an hour for the three hours we were out. Kuro was in great glee, for the weird appeals to him. "If we could only photograph by torchlight," he cried. But there was not much of the definiteness required in a picture. The water was dark, and the birds were dark all but their necks. The men handling the birds were merely silhouetted against the beacon. What light there was was fitful, and cast the blackest of shadows, that lost themselves in the near distance. We ourselves could not see the fish till the cormorants brought them up. We had a fine mess by the time we had gone the course, and were thoroughly gratified with our experience, but personally I should rather keep hounds than cormorants, having a prejudice against some odours.

The monkeys were the easiest game imaginable. The weapon used has laid many a good man low, but it is not a gun—it is saké. Monkeys like saké

NIGHT-FISHING IN JAPAN

quite as well as men like it and, like some men, they do not know when they have had enough. Kuro, Gardner, and I went into the hills with a guide who had a three-gallon cask of saké on his back and a dozen cups made from gourds. When we came to monkey town the guide set the bowls about under various trees and poured into each an inch or so of saké. Then we retired. I wished to stay by to watch, but the guide said if I did so the monkeys would know it, and I might wait until my beard grew to the ground—I should never see one. Probably he was right. At any rate when we returned we found four monkeys fast asleep and the twelve cups empty.

CHAPTER XXXIV

THE FATHER OF THE VILLAGE[1]

IT is hard to give up the fine things one is going to do—to leave the "big road" and hide one's self among the bypaths, but it is harder to give up what one has already accomplished—the thing that is done, which is a real possession; to give up the fruits of a long life; to lay aside a just reward when age has come upon one and it is too late to begin again.

But in Japan men can do this. Here is an instance. Gardner, Okashi, and I heard it one night from an aged fisherman whose grandfather was among the saved. It is the story of an old man who gave up what he had to save others, and afterwards the people worshipped him. The fisherman said the birth of this old hero was at a time of good omen.

"Shiawase no hito"; all the women said so, and they knew everything there was to know about

[1] The actual occurrence this story describes tells something of the native character. Lafcadio Hearn, whose wonderful sympathy with the Far East has given him so clear an insight to the soul of Japan, as well as a knowledge of the mind and of the spiritual aspirations of the people altogether unique, has used the incident in another guise in a delightful chapter.

THE FATHER OF THE VILLAGE 271

babies. Therefore was it true that the small, wrinkled, reddish thing given to the house of Hamaguchi early one morning, ere the great round harvest moon had set, was lucky. To be born by the light of the harvest moon is to be favoured of the gods. "Ii ambai," said the old women; "the way that is well"—which was the whole truth. After that each household in the hamlet understood the newcomer was "shiawase no hito" (one of those who are fortunate).

Hamaguchi no Bochan was a rare baby. Not because he seldom cried—all Japanese babies are too happy to cry; nor because he was gentle, for in this he was like all other merry, almond-eyed youngsters in the land where the sun rises; nor was it because he never had the colic, nor fussed about his teeth, nor kept a maid busy putting things right and cleaning up round the house and grounds wherever he had been. He was just like the other Japanese babies in these things too. But he had a baby dignity and wisdom that marked him.

He had as much fun as the jolliest of his playmates, who numbered probably a hundred. He was in all the games, and in all the mischief too; but somehow he was there as master, one whom the rest acknowledged. He did not squabble. Not even when he came to be a big boy, large enough to stand up with an oar in the sharp-pointed fishing-boats, did he order others about; but, nevertheless, the others did as he wished, and they liked to do so. It is not strange then that when he had grown to be a man and was the head of the Hamaguchi household, the people of the village made him "choja"—that is, chief or mayor.

As a husbandman he prospered. He raised rice for the villagers, whose chief business was on the sea, and they paid him in kind, for money was scarce in those days. What there was, was mostly in the strong box of the daimiyo of the province. This daimiyo owned all the villages within the boundaries of his dominion. The rice the farmers raised, and all the fish that men caught in their nets were his. Whatever portion he was pleased to allow them they took, and the rest he held as taxes to maintain himself, his castles, and his fighting-men.

The head of the house of Hamaguchi grew rice on thousands of tsubo of the daimiyo's land, and paid him many koku of his produce at harvest-time in tithes and rents and tributes, but the koku that remained to the choja were more than the portion of any other person in the village. A koku of rice in those days was well-nigh the year's income of some folk, though it seems hard a man should have to live twelve months on what he can sell five bushels of grain for in the market.

Choja Sama was generous with his abundance, and gave freely to those who had not; so freely, indeed, that at each year's end when the day of accounting came he found he had used all the yielding of his fields—the greater part had gone to the daimiyo and the rest to his household and to the other villagers.

This was so, no matter how large the harvest might be, but it did not matter, Choja Sama did not think of it. He was a favoured one. Always, both

THE FATHER OF THE VILLAGE 273

in spring and autumn, his crops were good; always he had enough to satisfy even the steward of the great lord who ruled the ken, enough for his home and for all who called him "choja." So as "shiawase no hito" the folk spoke of him who was now the father of fair daughters and brave sons—a man of dignity and gentleness and wisdom, who ruled the village well and served his daimiyo loyally.

What more could he be? He certainly had no thought of anything. His people's happiness was all he cared for. Nor could those who knew him believe he had not all that a dweller in a humble fishing village could acquire. But greater honour came upon him nevertheless. He became a god, and his people worshipped him.

It was when he was well along in years, a grey-haired man, in the evening of his days. On an evening of this evening he did the great deed of his life. Although for a long time he had been "inkiyo," or retired, and his son had succeeded to the active head of the household, he was too much alive to give himself up to poetry and meditation, and had continued to be the head of village affairs and to oversee the rice-fields rented from the daimiyo.

It was again the time of the harvest moon, near four-score years since the old women had stood by and greeted him with prophecies of the favours that should be his through life. The crops were in, and the yellow stacks stood high about the choja's home near the temple on the hill. There was a festival in the village in honour of the Goddess of Good Luck—she of the round, merry, dimpled face, and of the

Gods of Wealth and Plenty—corpulent deities with fat ears, koku of rice stacked high, and piles of gold pieces.

The fishermen and the few who were farmers, with their wives and families, and the singing and dancing girls, or geisha, were making merry within and round about their sacred tera, high above the beach, when someone cried, "Chotto go ran nasai! Shiwo ga hiku taihen desu!" ("Look for a moment, the tide is gone far out!") And so it was, and seemed going farther still. Everyone arose, and, after wondering for a moment, ran down to the beach below and far out towards the receding waters.

That is, everyone went down but Choja Sama. He was old, and besides he knew something of low tides and that they boded ill for the coast where they appeared. "This ebb was so very low, what would the return of the waters be?" he thought to himself.

Though the moon was up, that glorious golden moon in the deep, full blue sky of Japan, the sun hardly had set, and the last rays still flitted lingeringly across the bosom of the sea. The old man looked down and saw his people away out beyond the natural limits of the beach. He could hear their shouts and laughter—deafness is rare even with the aged in Japan—and his heart was heavy with fear. He looked towards the spot where the sun had set, and away almost to the horizon, it seemed, was a fine strip of light that glistened and moved towards him.

"Nami," he said, "O nami." And so it was, a great wave coming to the shore, a wave so great it had

THE FATHER OF THE VILLAGE

sucked the sea away from the land and piled it up in a wall like a mountain range. It was a tidal-wave, such as an earthquake beneath the waters of the ocean makes sometimes and sends against the coast to smite it as the very wrath of God.

This is what Choja Sama saw, and he saw, too, that before he could climb down with his aged limbs and reach his people to give them warning, that awful wall of water would be upon them and they would be lost. There was no time to think—only to act.

He was standing by the house in which he had lived since he was born. Almost touching the walls, on the windward side, were the stacks of rice his sons and their helpers had finished harvesting the day before. There were the portions for the lord of the province and for his own use and for the needy ones. All of this he must have, to settle the accounts of the business of the year. To have this grain threshed and safely in the village warehouse meant prosperity and comfort; but in a moment it was crackling fiercely, blazing high over the hilltop, and sending a glare down upon the startled villagers below, who turned together as one person and rushed landward, looking up and crying that their choja was burning in his house and must be saved.

Great was their amazement when they reached the hilltop to see the old man standing by watching the fire calmly as it consumed his home and the produce of his fields—leaving him without a roof to shelter him and making him a debtor to his lord for the remainder of his years. A charred bamboo pole was in his hands, which he had used to feed the flames. The people thought him mad.

He had not looked up at their coming, so busy he had been, but now he turned toward them and pointed to the sea. They were dumb, but had they all cried at once, and to their utmost, their voices would not have sounded even in their own ears. The waters had returned, and the crested wave, reaching up thirty feet above the beach, had broken, washing away the fishers' huts along the shore as houses built of cards would go. It receded and returned, and again drew back to flood a third time. When it had finished this last assault, night was upon the place and the village had disappeared. The harvest moon looked down on a place where one had been, and on a crowd of frightened fisherfolk huddled round the ruins of the home of an old man for whom, later, when they had recovered from their wonder and had mortgaged their belongings, they built a temple and worshipped as Hamaguchi Daimiyojin. So was he, even at the last, "shiawase no hito."

CHAPTER XXXV

THE THEFT OF THE GOLDEN SCALE

OKASHI KINTARO was gazing into his saké cup reflectively. It was a cup with pictures on it — two views of the same subject; the front presentation on the inside of the cup, and the other on the bottom — a cup such as you have sometimes when cooling on the dry bed of Kamogawa in Kiyoto if you happen to be on good terms with those who serve you, but which you never leave with your other curios for Custom House inspection on reaching home.

"That inside picture seems to interest you," said Gardner. "Do you recognise the face?" The reply and the story following, Okashi told in language all his own, to this effect:—

"The countenance resembles that of Daredesuka's sweetheart, but I never saw it on a saké cup before."

"Daredesuka?"

"Yes, the man who tried to steal gold from the shachi hoko on the tenshu in Nagoya."

"The which on the what?"

"The great gold dolphins on the ends of the ridge of Nagoya Castle. General Kato Kiyomasa put them up there nearly three hundred years ago, quite out of harm's way you would think."

"Yes, I remember you pointed out the fish a little before we reached Nagoya Station on our way through; but tell us about Daredesuka and his sweetheart. What did they do?"

"Daredesuka was a samurai who had been with the daimiyo of Kaga once, and had won fame as a great swordsman. But when the daimiyo died Daredesuka became "ronin"; that is, a samurai without a master. He went about teaching fencing, and sometimes winning prizes in contests before distinguished folk, but never getting established anywhere. He was too fond of roaming. He used to practise with his sword on all the forked limbs of trees that he could reach, and also on the wild dogs that are as dangerous as wolves on the west coast roads. It is said that once when robbers tried to take him he cut through two bodies with a single stroke, and that the other robbers seeing this ran away, crying that he was an "Oni" (demon) not a man.

"In time he came to Kiyoto, which was a larger city then, and was the home of the Tenshi, our Emperor. The Shogun lived in Yedo—this was a long time before the name was changed to Tokio. Soon after Daredesuka arrived, the Shogun came down to Kiyoto to see the Tenshi. He had to come once a year, according to ancient custom. Of course this meant a great deal of preparation. The ceremonies were elaborate, and the court nobles, who usually were poor, made money by teaching the proper etiquette to the Shogun's officers. Geisha

THE THEFT OF THE GOLDEN SCALE 279

were busy in all the tea-houses, and gathered gold pieces enough to last them a whole month, which is a long time when speaking of geisha. There were all sorts of sport too—polo, archery on horseback, fencing, and "jiujutsu," which is a kind of wrestling.

"Daredesuka was the right kind of man for such a time. He went into many contests and won so often that the people talked about him in the streets. Because he was a winner he became the guest at many banquets, and did not have to buy any food himself for several weeks. At the banquets he saw many geisha, who came to dance and to sing and to play, just as they are doing over yonder now," pointing to a tea-house all open on one side along the river bank.

"Being a military man, Daredesuka did not care much for geisha. He had the name of a strict and severe man. One night, however, at a chaya just at the end of this bridge, the most famous tea-house of all in Kiyoto, Daredesuka changed his idea.

"Eikibo San was the cause of the change. She was a geisha who did the fan dancing most famously, and was never engaged except in the best houses and by the richest guests. When Daredesuka saw her dancing he could not look from her. She swayed this way and that way gently as a lily when the autumn wind is blowing, and her fan went round her like a butterfly that she had trained. Her face was white except the colour of cherry blossoms on the cheeks, and her eyebrows high as in the pictures on these fans. Her hands were long and fine, and waved like birds' wings when she turned about, playing and tossing with the fan. So long and so hard was Daredesuka looking that the soups and fishes the other geisha were serving to him became quite cold, and some of the guests near by were wondering. Then one of these said—

"'You have never seen Eikibo San before? She is our best dancer. Even the Shogun, they say, has seen her. Many men have tried to take her home, but she does not listen. She has no lover. She lives with an old aunt, as she calls her, in the geisha quarter, and never leaves the old woman alone for a single night, nor does she ever respond to any callers who go there to give her presents. These gift-bearers talk with the old aunt at the gate, but no one of them has ever had his foot inside.'

"This, if it could be, made Daredesuka even keener, so that when the fan dancing was over and Eikibo came round to do her turn at pouring saké, beginning before him as the chief guest, he said she must first drink from his cup, and might afterwards serve him. She took the dainty bit of porcelain from him, and bowing low, touched it to her forehead. Then Daredesuka poured saké from the china bottle in front of him, but could give her only a few drops, as she pushed the mouth of the bottle up with the edge of the cup, saying, 'More would be a great deal.' She made as though she drank it, but one could not tell, for the geisha is skilful to pretend. Then, before she could rinse the cup, Daredesuka took it from her and said, 'Ippai dozo gomen nasai' ('Full please and excuse me').

"Eikibo laughed because he did not let her rinse

THE THEFT OF THE GOLDEN SCALE 281

the cup. Then she passed on to the next guest, reaching out the saké bottle with her arm at full length and her sleeve caught up between her teeth out of the way of the soup bowls and other dishes on the mat before her.

"After this everything was different for Daredesuka. He wished to see Eikibo San every day and all day long. That could not be, but if he kept his fame he might see her at the tea-house festivals while the Shogun remained in Kiyoto, and after that, if he could get money, he could call on her by himself, he hoped.

"He kept his fame for the remaining contests. Perhaps he made it even greater, for he had an offer to go with a great daimiyo to the south, who promised him a post as instructor of his retainers and many koku of rice with a home and servants. Before the fan dancing he would have gone, I am sure, had such a good chance come, but now he could not travel far and leave Eikibo San behind.

"As he could not take her on the daimiyo's train he made humble apologies, and said that so great honour could not be his for he had made an agreement already with another to travel farther north. There was more truth than he thought in this, for he did go from Kiyoto later and along the road that takes one north. He did not mean to when he declined this offer though.

"Five or six times after this Daredesuka saw Eikibo before the Shogun left, always in the same tea-house and with the same few words, for he could not detain her beyond the drinking of a single cup of saké. She would apologise and say that there were many guests and too few to wait on them, therefore she must not stay long. After the Shogun had set out on his return to Yedo, Daredesuka called the geisha several times from a quiet tea-house down the river, but only once she came, for her engagements almost never failed. Her name was on some lists for months ahead.

"As soon as the maids had brought refreshments and retired he made an offer to her which almost always a geisha will accept. She should be his wife. He would take service with some quiet daimiyo within the next six months, and she would then be in the highest of the four classes of society and ranking almost as one of the nobility. He told her of offers he had received and had refused because he could not bear to leave her, and said he would accept whichever one she chose if she would come with him.

"Eikibo laughed at all this, being, she said, familiar with fine promises. 'They are all of a kind,' she told him; 'interesting to hear, if you did not know they were like little flies that live a day and then no one knows what has become of them.' Daredesuka persisted, but only to find that words did not avail. At last he cried—

"'Give me some test, for I must have you know that I speak truth. Shall I bring you pearls from the deep sea or golden scales from the dolphins on Nagoya Castle? Only say the thing and I shall do it. You shall believe me.'

"Eikibo looked merrily at him, and said—

THE THEFT OF THE GOLDEN SCALE

"'Yes, I must believe you if you bring me a dolphin's golden scale from the ridge of the fifth storey of the tower, as I know well, for I am in Nagoya every year. Only the birds go up there. Yes, I should know you spoke the truth if you brought the scale'; and she laughed again, for to the geisha the truthful parents of the truthful man are not yet born. Then she added: 'My call time for the Full Moon tea-house over the river has arrived. I beg your honourable pardon. I must go. At the great matsuri' (religious festival) 'in Nagoya next month I am to dance. Bring me the scale then, and I shall know your heart.'

"Daredesuka sat still for an hour thinking, and then, as the samurai often did on the night before the battle, he clapped his hands, ordered more saké and more food, sent to an inn near by for a friend who was lodging there, and made merry until the watch announced the hour for closing. Two nights later he was in Nagoya.

"As you know, those gold fishes are high up, and perhaps you could see that each is now in a heavy cage. That cage was not there in Daredesuka's time. You know, too, that we Japanese enjoy our play with kites. We can send them very high and can guide them nicely. Well, Daredesuka was a wonderful man with kites. He had made large ones when he was with his late lord, and had once dropped a line far out over a junk that was blowing off to sea, and so saved many lives. He now said he would use a kite to get the scale that Eikibo had declared would tell if he spoke true. Secretly he went to work, and made one so large he was sure it would carry the weight of his body on the wind. He found another ronin whom some gold and the promise of future aid persuaded to give him help in his strange plan. Then on a stormy night, with wind and clouds and rain, he went up and secured a golden scale. But the tool he had used in prying was very wet and slippery and fell from his hands. The guards went out and discovered the kite, which a rift in the sky let the moon shine down upon for a fatal moment, and when he reached the earth they caught him and put him in prison. The golden scale convicted him and his companion. Being samurai they received sentence to comit hara-kiri, and they performed the act serenely before the State officials.

"Eikibo did not do the fan dance at the matsuri, for on the morning of the day she was to appear an old priest found her body on Daredesuka's grave."

CHAPTER XXXVI

THE KANJI

I WAS living in a charming missionary family in Tsukiji, wishing I could be a missionary too. (This was before Gardner had come to the Land of the Rising Sun.) It was one of those mornings one sees only in Japan. There was such glorious satisfaction in the air that one was quite too happy to think of work.

As I contemplated the peacefulness of everything, the joy of being absolutely idle and equally as happy, I heard a clatter at the door below. Then Seikichi, the hall boy, came up to the music-room where I had arranged a temporary studio and announced—

"Honourable guest augustly waits in honourable reception room."

"Ah! honourable he does?" queried I. "Who the deuce augustly is he?" I did not like the racket he had made. It had disturbed my contemplation. Why had not he pressed the button?

"Honourable guest, honourable name card has not," replied Seikichi with a low bow, and I thought the suspicion of a grin. Then he explained that the caller came from a school up on Surugadai, near the

Greek cathedral. He was "kanji," or business manager, of this school.

"Perhaps the school is looking for a teacher," I said to myself. "I should like to see it." I knew Surugadai. It was about the highest point in Tokio. From the scaffolding of the cathedral I had seen the entire capital by merely turning on my heel and looking straight before me. Even the province of Suruga, ninety miles away, was visible. Hence the name "Suruga-dai," or terrace. Really I hoped the kanji wished to engage me.

As I went down I heard more clatter, but I soon ascertained it was only the honourable guest calling for tobacco, which the reverend owner of the house, in violence to the custom of the country, had neglected to put on his free list.

Looking through the door of the reception-room I spied the kanji sitting on his shins amongst the chairs, which seemingly he disdained, looking about for the tobacco jar that was not there, and pounding a footstool the while to attract the attention of someone who might minister to his wants.

"May I have the honour to be of service to you?" I ventured.

"I wish smoking," he replied; and then jumping up he put out his hand, saying—

"How do you do I am very well I thank you yes sir I think so myself." Which was rather good for one breath. Then he replenished himself with air by an indrawn hiss that must have appropriated a good two gallons of the Tsukiji atmosphere. Handing him a cigar I waited for him to continue the conversation

THE KANJI

which he had begun so cleverly himself, but he needed a match first, and then a clip to bite the top off with, and a tip as to which end to bite, before he could go on. He was not quite into New Japan yet, though he had made some progress in getting out of the Old.

"Sir," he said at last, "our name are Ojigoku Kitsune. Our business are the Kanji of Atama no Nakakara school on Surugadai's top and our desire is you come every days for the teaching by the English languages and the improvement to the mind for the many scholars and female ladies and boy." Then he hissed in air again.

By the way his words came out I was sure he had written them down and committed them to memory. I was right, for here he hesitated and began feeling in his pockets for his "crib." It took him some time to find it, and as he searched I inventoried his appearance. His face was stubbly and suggestive of a fox, his eyes rounder and a trifle lighter than is usual with Japanese, and his hair was of the same length all over, and stuck out straight from his head like fretful quills. This was due to much early shaving of the poll.

His coat was of the full frock, or "Prince Albert" cut, the material was alpaca. When he unbuttoned it he discovered a waistcoat suitable for evening dress, and also the upper half of a shirt-front to which the ingenious constructer thereof had affixed a collar and a bright green tie. The tie had worked round under the coat collar or I might have noticed it before. What was between him and that shirt-front I could only guess. It might have been a liver pad with sleeve attachments. His trousers were linen, but whether the right leg or the left leg preserved the original shade I could not say. There was a marked difference between the two. As he had taken off his shoes on entering the house I noticed that he wore mittens on his feet.

When he had found his crib he puckered up his mouth again and said—

"How do you do—er O ah—no, I am mistaken." He had started at the beginning again, like an interrupted cathedral guide. Farther down he found the place, and read—

"The hour shall be paid the dollar and the transportation to the school and to the house." A dollar an hour and a jin-riki-sha from home to school and back again is what he meant. I did not agree to quite those terms, but eventually I said I would visit Surugadai to promote the knowledge among all the students, including " and boy."

When I said I would go, he replied—

"Yes, I think so myself." Then putting on his hat, a fore-and-aft arrangement like an inverted "pram," he pushed his mittens into his shoes, pocketed his cigar, and disappeared.

While at tiffin two days later, Seikichi announced—

"Jin-riki-sha from Surugadai."

He smiled as he spoke, and I understood when I was outside. There was the man-power-cart, all but the man. Instead of man there was a midget of the size the factories pay a penny a day for now. Quite useless for a grade either up or down, for he weighed a quarter of what I did. However, I let him pull me on the levels, and he was not half bad.

The next time he called for me, Mrs. Gazell, the missionary's wife, happened to be giving instructions to the cook at the rear, where the midget waited until I had finished tiffin. When she came in she said—

"Your insect has arrived. He is buzzing in the kitchen now. I hope he doesn't stick in any of the sweets!"

From that time on Tsukiji knew him as my "mushi" (mushi is Japanese for insect).

Mushi and I got on very well together. Whenever we came to an incline I jumped out and let him rattle along by himself. On the way home he took me to the shops along the Ginza, where usually I had some household commissions to attend to, and then I would buy him an egg to suck, in the hope that he would grow. One evening when I reached home I found a professor of Atama no Nakakara waiting for my mushi. He had walked over from the Ginza, a mile out of his way, and had been waiting an hour to save threepence, the fare from a Ginza jin-riki-sha stand to Surugadai.

On my next visit to the school, Kitsune the Kanji addressed me elaborately on the subject of jin-riki-sha.

"Sir," he said, "from the school to the home and the jin-riki-sha not stopping is for the agreement."

"You did not mention anything about time or route when you said you would furnish the jin-riki-sha," I replied.

"Yes, but the man being only the small boy, by the long distances are very tiresome."

"He is resting while I am in the shops," I said, "and Ginza is not a very indirect route home."

"But he wishes times for eatings or he catch the stomach illness."

"I give him eggs, won't they do?" I asked.

Here the kanji disappeared for a few minutes. When he returned he said—

"Honourable egg are good but it is necessity for the fish and rice."

"But you did not mention fish and rice nor say I should feed the infant when you engaged me."

"Yes, but he have the unhealth and are not powerful to transport the long distances."

"Get a man then."

Here the kanji made another disappearance. On coming out again he said:

"Sir, every days four sen (1d.) you are giving for the eating and we are adjust."

"But I understood you to say that the infant has the unhealth."

"Yes," replied the kanji, "but he have become strong."

I had nothing to say.

All went well until the end of the month, when the payment agreed upon was due me. The kanji came into the classroom and said—

"The money is come to-morrow by the bank for closing is too early to-day." The bank closing, he meant.

"You will come to Tsukiji?"

THE KANJI

" Oh, I am doubtless. I am Christian."

"Yes? You had not told me so before. I shall be away by nine o'clock. Will you call earlier?"

" I before nine time—sure."

" The bank will be open before nine o'clock?"

"Yes, the bank is close perhaps but we shall do the arrangement by the night."

Well, in the morning the kanji came: alpaca frock-coat, green tie, inverted pram, and all—all but my salary, that is. He said he had started out with the full amount, but on the way down he saw some things he needed, and "therefore we are spend parts. I am return it pleasantly." (Meaning presently, for he had learned the sound of "l" and, being proud of the accomplishment, rather overworked it.)

"Yes," I replied, "perhaps you will, but I shall be at Surugadai this afternoon and shall see the Principal. Perhaps he will arrange the matter."

The kanji smiled and went away. I never saw him again, but Atama no Nakakara made good his deficit.

CHAPTER XXXVII

THE REVERENCE OF KATO

FOR a man to reverence his father and his mother is a grand thing. In the Far East the fifth commandment is the law of laws; folk obey it with a fervour that Westerners can hardly understand. Their zeal calls to mind one of Freeman's words anent the chivalry of knights who made arbitrary choice of some one virtue which they practised with such enthusiasm that it became a vice, while they neglected the ordinary laws of right and wrong entirely.

In China, for example, the "great calamity" is that ancestors should lack descendants to do them honour. This idea led long ago to plural wives and "the devil in the household." In Japan ancestors and even step-ancestors came to be supreme. All other relations were trifling compared to the attitude of son to father, and an Abraham offering up Isaac would be a small matter beside some acts of "filial piety" in the Land of the Rising Sun, for a Japanese has sacrificed not only a son but his whole family and himself to do the bidding of his adopted father. The story will show this better than a volume

THE REVERENCE OF KATO 293

of essays on what Confucius taught concerning reverence.

Years ago in the province of Owari, near the centre of Japan, lived Kato Tamakichi, a potter. Kato went through with a difficult enterprise successfully, and won for his countrymen great fame. In this achievement duty was the only stimulus, for the reward he knew he should receive was not attractive.

Seto was Kato Tamakichi's native town. In his time it was the centre of the porcelain industry of the Empire, as it is to-day. Indeed it has been the centre ever since his famous ancestor Kato Shirozemon returned from China seven centuries ago with the store of knowledge he had gleaned during his years of study among the ancient kilns.

And now "Setomono" (Seto-things), is a generic term in Japanese for all pottery and porcelain, just as "china" is in English. But though descended from a long line of masters of the kiln in a country where potters had great honour, and though he was the cleverest of the pupils of his master, Tsugane Bunzaemon, chief of the Seto Guild of Potters, was not content. A stranger looking in on him would not have suspected his discontent, perhaps, for the Japanese face is wonderfully effective as a mask, but the discontent was there.

Kato Tamakichi was at his home one day in his master's house. He had knelt down, and seated himself on his heels by a large bronze hibachi, making ready to put the kettle on for a little tea. Before him were several tea-bowls, delicate and beautiful in design and of exquisite glaze.

This glaze was the cause of Kato's discontent. Tsugane San had just returned from his voyage round Cape Shiwo to Osaka, where he went each year to visit the great bazaars, which at that time were the largest in the Empire, and to dispose of the product of the Seto kilns, and had brought back with him these tea-bowls.

They were so good they worried the young potter. He would pause, fire-tongs in hand, every moment or two, pick up one of the bowls, hold it between his eye and the light, put a coal close to it to study the glow reflected from the surface, rub it along his sleeve, touch it gingerly with the tip of his tongue as though to taste the deep rich colour under the glaze, tap it very, very gently with one of the long tips, and then set it down again and become absorbed in the arrangement of the fire.

Tsugane San came in shortly and seated himself upon a square cushion on the opposite side of the hibachi. He pulled the tea-tray towards him, and taking the tall blue cup—the master's cup—poured a little hot water in it and replaced it on the tray. Opening an air-tight canister which had a lid with a rim quite half as deep as the canister's entire height he took out two pinches of tea, dried leaves of a deep dull green that had never suffered from other heat or chemical process than the sun's rays effect. The two pinches went into the "kibisho," or small porcelain teapot. Next he poured boiling water from the "tetsubin," the iron tea-kettle, into a sort of gravy boat, where it must cool a bit, lest it make the brew astringent. Replacing the tea-kettle on the brazier, he turned the moderated boiling water on the leaves, let it stand perhaps a minute, and pouring a tiny cup half full for Kato San, his cup full for himself, drank the sherry-coloured liquor slowly with a sound somewhere between a kiss and a sigh.

Kato San drank with him, and when he had done the master said—

"As for those tea-bowls from Osaka, what do you think?"

"Augustly beautiful," replied Kato, using the honorific form, out of the respect a pupil should always show to his master.

"Yes, beautiful they are. Too beautiful for Osaka —too beautiful for Seto. They are from far south, as you see by their bottoms, from Arita and Karatsu, in the province of Hizen, where the Prince of Satsuma settled some Koreans a hundred years ago and made them teach the natives many things about enamels. There is good stone there for porcelain, and the ports of Karatsu and of Imari, where the Dutch send every year for wares, has become as famous in Kiushiu as our Seto is in the remainder of Dai Nippon. In fact, those southerners call everything of clay, Karatsumono. They are pushing their wares north now. I had a hard time selling in Osaka this visit, and all because those low Koreans whom we conquer so easily whenever we cross the channel had a secret about glaze which they were fools enough to tell the potters in Hizen."

"Honourably augustly so it contemptibly deigns

to be," said Kato San, inclining his head and bending forward.

"We must discover that secret," continued the master.

To which Kato San assented with more honorifics and inclinations.

In Osaka I saw a "nakado" (middleman) who has gone to Hizen to arrange for a marriage with the daughter of the chief of the Arita Guild. It will cost all of the year's profits and something besides, but we shall lose our face if we do not discover the secret of the glaze."

Respectful acquiescence as before.

"From what I learned through Nakado San I am confident of success. He will be here within a few days and will return with you directly, for it is a long journey and I would have you be there before the next firing of the kilns."

This was the first intimation of Tsugane San's scheme that had reached Kato San; it was in fact the first time the subject of marriage had been mentioned to him, but he bowed quite as reverently as before and ejaculated honorifics in the same deferential tone. On his countenance there was no sign that he had just heard he was to go to a strange country there to marry a strange woman whose speech even would be unintelligible. But Japanese surprise, if there is such a thing, is purely internal. Tsugane San had made arrangements, and that was the affair in a nutshell. Why discuss matters that are already settled?

In due course Nakado San appeared with a letter

THE REVERENCE OF KATO

showing that he had done all as Tsugane San had instructed him, so nothing remained for him to do except to receive the money stipulated and then hasten back with Kato San to Arita where the potters were waiting eagerly' to celebrate. Kato received money, too, and handsome gifts for the wife he had never seen and for her parents. As Tsugane handed these to his pupil and adopted son, he said—

"When you have learned the blue and white, return."

And Kato, with his forehead against the mats, had replied—

"Kashikomarimashita" ("August commands reverently understanding am ").

Then with his guide he set out, hardly daring to look about him on the sights he had known since the light first shone upon him. Their luggage was partly on the backs of two lusty coolies and partly in their "kagos," or palanquins, for Kato had small liking to be carried along the road. He preferred exercise. Nagoya, where the golden dolphins are, was their first halt, about six "ri" (fifteen miles) from home. Thence they went on to Kokkaichi, thence over the mountains to Lake Biwa, and to Kiyoto where the Son of Heaven, Tenshi Sama, the Mikado, was a sacred prisoner by order of the Shogun Tauna Yoshi; on to Osaka, where more business was done more slowly than in any other city in Japan; thence by boat through the wondrous Inland Sea which angels look down upon with envy; through the Strait of Shimonoseki, where allied Western fleets were to meet years afterwards, and into the "Genkai Nada" (the Watchful Sea), to Karatsu, where the men of Arita met them as Nakado San had arranged.

As Kato San had left his own home and was coming to the bride's house to become a member of her family, which is just the reverse of what usually occurs when young folks marry in Japan, and as, furthermore, the homes of bride and bridegroom were far apart, as distances went in those days, the Nakado altered the ordinary arrangements to suit the circumstances. He arranged the "mi-ai" (mutual seeing or first look) to take place in rooms he had rented near Arita for the purpose. It was satisfactory, of course, it always is with dutiful children in Japan, and in those days before knowledge of Western ways had reached the country there was none other in Japan.

It is true the young people sat at opposite sides of the room with many mats between them, and that neither ventured a word to the other directly, but Kato's fine features, his clear keen eye, as an artist should have, and his erectness, all of which O Tsuru San saw without looking at their possessor, put her into a most pleasurable confusion; while as for Kato himself, he looked directly at O Tsuru as she came in, and from that moment forgot his home-sickness entirely.

The ceremony of "San San Kudo" (Three Three Nine Times) where bride and bridegroom go through the form of exchanging each of three saké cups three times, and drinking, was in the bride's house two days later, where Kato took the name of Higashidori from his father-in-law, whose son he now became, and

THE REVERENCE OF KATO

was duly registered at the office of the district by the census taker as Higashidori Tokuzayemon, chief of the Arita Guild of Potters.

It seems that Rei Sampei had just discovered some fine porcelain stone in Idzumi Yama, and the kilns had better clay in them than they had ever known before. Higashidori, too, had added to the knowledge the Koreans had brought over through his dealings with the Dutch, whom the Shogun allowed once a year to do a little business at Deshima, Nagasaki. His skill with red oxide of iron and with Chinese and Dutch cobalt gave him the advantage that Tsugane Bunzaemon had envied so keenly. Under the catalogue title "Old Hizen," in the Dresden collection, one may see specimens of Higashidori's skill to-day.

Kato San, skilful as he was himself, marvelled at the work of his new father and set about diligently to assist him. Being a potter born and bred, he was soon in love with his occupation, almost half as much as he was with his wife, which is saying a great deal. Higashidori smiled as he watched his son, and thought what a fine man he would be when age came on and it was time for the headship of the guild to pass on to one of a younger generation.

"I shall be 'inkiyo' (retired) then," he said to himself, "and Kintaro will have the kilns and will be chief in my stead. He will be worthy of our name."

When, a year later, O Tsuru San presented her husband with a son the old chief's countenance was lighted with a joy that shone more brightly than the finest vases he had ever made. The bond between him and the son from far away was now complete, and the honour of his house secure. He took Kintaro into his full confidence, and the young man learning rapidly was soon well-nigh as expert as the chief himself. His work delighted him, and his home, to which two more children came in the next three years, was all that a human heart could wish for. So absorbed had he become in the development of the porcelains from the new-found stone, that Seto and the master waiting there were as dim shadows in his mind, if ever he thought of them at all.

But a stranger to Arita passed through one day, leaving a written message with Kintaro, and affairs changed. It was from Tsugane Bunzaemon, the master. Kintaro turned to stone on reading it. It was a clear, fine day, but he did not know it. A few feet from him two of his children were playing at battledore and shuttlecock, he did not hear them. On the mats just beyond the shallow grooves along which the sliding doors had been pushed back, making an entrance to the adjoining room, O Tsuru San sat nursing the youngest of the three—a lovely picture of young motherhood, but Kintaro did not see.

He folded the letter and went out and over to the quarry, then he walked to the kilns, and then—he never knew himself where he wandered during the next few hours, but his thoughts were on the serving of two masters, one whom he had forgotten and the other whom he had come to look upon as in very truth his father.

"Yet he is not," he murmured to himself. "My real father, who died when I was so young, gave me to the master, for he wished me to grow up to be famous among the Seto kilns, as he was himself. I kept his name, and I must be true to him—as he would have it;—that—is—true—to—Seto,—and these four years are gone, and the end of them and of me is near."

"Of them"—the tragedy of the thoughts that came with those two words!

Kintaro thought things over many ways and slowly as he wandered. Then, his mind being clear, he said to Higashidori—

"You are to become inkiyo soon and retire from all active pursuits, as your honourable years entitle you to do, and as you have had the august condescension to name so unworthy a person as I to be your heir and successor, I beg you to allow me a short visit to my former home that I may say farewell to the comrades of my early youth whom I shall otherwise have no opportunity to see again."

The journey was speedily arranged. Kintaro bowed low to Higashidori, put his hand on the children's heads as he asked them which could strike the shuttlecock the farther, and just for a moment touched the hem of O Tsuru's sleeve, as he said he must hasten lest a waiting junk make sail before he reached the harbour.

He did not see them again, nor Arita neither. Ten months later news came that the Seto kilns produced all the glaze and colourings that had made Hizen so famous, and that the new Seto had monopolised the markets in Osaka. In their rage the Arita potters crucified Kintaro's wife and his children. Kintaro—or

Kato Tamakichi—when the story reached him became a raving maniac. In Seto his memory is sacred, for he had obeyed the commands of the master to whom his father had committed him. Filial piety had its reward.

For Product Safety Concerns and Information please contact our EU
representative GPSR@taylorandfrancis.com
Taylor & Francis Verlag GmbH, Kaufingerstraße 24, 80331 München, Germany

www.ingramcontent.com/pod-product-compliance
Lightning Source LLC
Chambersburg PA
CBHW060551230426
43670CB00011B/1776